Newspapers

K. JOHN WESTMANCOAT

The British Library

For Helen

© 1985 The British Library Board

Published by
The British Library
Reference Division Publications
Great Russell Street
London WC1B 3DG

and 51 Washington Street,
Dover, New Hampshire 03820

British Library Cataloguing in
Publication Data

Westmancoat, K. John
    Newspapers.
    1. Newspapers——History
    I. Title   II. British Library
    070.1'72'09   PN4801

    ISBN 0–7123–0055–4

Library of Congress Cataloging in
Publication Data

Westmancoat, K. John.
    Newspapers.

    Bibliography: P.
    1. English newspapers – history. I.
British Library. II. Title.
PN5114.W43 1985   072   85–1
8980
    ISBN 0–7123–0055–4 (Pbk.)

Front cover. B R Haydon,
'Waiting for *the Times*'. ©
Times Newspapers Limited.
Reprinted, by permission.

Back cover. The Gentlewoman,
Christmas Number 1899.

Designed by Roger Davies
Typeset in Monophoto Ehrhardt by
August Filmsetting, Haydock,
St. Helens
Origination by York House Graphics,
Hanwell
Printed and bound in Great Britain by
William Clowes Ltd, Beccles

A true Representation of a Printing Hou

Engraved for the New Univers

the Men at Work.

zine 1752.   *B.Cole sculp.*

Contents

"THE GENTLEWOMAN" Copyright.

His Royal Highness
The Prince of Wales, K.G.

"THE GENTLEWOMAN" Copyright.

Her Royal Highness
The Princess of Wales.

Introduction

The daily appearance of newspapers exhibiting varied political viewpoints is an accepted sign of a free press. As long as the publication is not libellous, obscene or deemed likely to endanger national security, the editor of a newspaper published in a democratic society is permitted a free hand. This has not always been so. Journalists today may be asked to reveal their sources, but it is only comparatively recently in the history of printing that printers have not been imprisoned, sentenced to the pillory or heavily fined for almost any unguarded statement.

The earliest printers had to fight for this freedom, which had been denied them since the introduction by Johann Gutenberg of printing with movable type. One form of censorship, imposed by the Catholic Church in Europe, was eventually replaced in England by one enforced by the King's ministers, spiritual and temporal, through the Star Chamber. Church and State made use of the printing press; but both found that the power wielded by it was difficult to control, even by means of repressive decrees and the later introduction of a newspaper stamp tax.

This is still the situation today in countries where the State controls the press and thereby ensures that specific national or party policies are followed or extolled through the pages of carefully regulated articles. In some Latin American countries and in the USSR censorship is practised and has been in force for so long that the art has been refined. The other media – radio, television and news agencies – are also tightly controlled. If one extends the analogy to a democracy it is easy for certain minority interest groups to argue that their views are not represented by the presses of big business. An undefined censorship is said to exist, with the result that the phenomenon of the 'alternative' press has taken on a new prominence over the last twenty years. In many respects, however, alternative titles such as *Oz* or *Gay News*, which were subject to prosecution in the 1970s, are only the late 20th century equivalents of *The Anarchist, Poor Man's Guardian, Chartist Circular*, or unstamped working-class periodicals published during the 19th century. Each represents the viewpoint of a new generation, rebelling against a society whose values are not acceptable.

A problem for newspaper historians is that not all alternative titles have readily found their way into the major collections, such as those of the British Library, because some publishers neglect to comply with legal deposit regulations. Thus scholars are deprived of an important source of research material which may, in years to come, rival Thomason's collection of tracts and newsbooks from the English Civil War as social documents.

1, 2 Free gifts are not a modern phenomenon. Victorian and Edwardian coloured portraits printed on silk or satin have been kept by subsequent generations. This type of print was expensive to produce. Many were commissioned from German printers. (*The Gentlewoman*, Christmas numbers, 1899 and 1900.)

3 The forerunner of the computer dating service. Honourable intentions were expressed publicly in the *Matrimonial Post*, published from 1860 to 1955. (*Matrimonial Post*, February 1912.)

4 *right. The Suffragette* was one of several newspapers which were published during the long, violent and sometimes fatal struggle for female enfranchisement in Britain. (*The Suffragette*, 18 October 1912.)

5 *overleaf left. Woman's Own* has not lost its appeal over the last five decades. Although the price has increased, this weekly periodical retains a proven combination of interesting feature articles, fiction, handicrafts, sound advice and appetizing recipes. (*Woman's Own*, 15 October 1932.)

6 *overleaf right.* Korky the Cat is as popular with the children of the 1980s as he was in 1937. *The Dandy* is just one of the many famous comics in the Newspaper Library's collections. (*The Dandy*, 4 December 1937.) © D. C. Thomson Ltd.

These tracts and Dr Charles Burney's collections of London newspapers published between 1603 and 1817, all now in the British Library, are acknowledged as extremely useful sources for scholars. The Library's extensive provincial, Scottish, Irish and overseas collections provide the opportunity to study the past, and to develop a stimulating acquaintance with the flesh and blood of history which cannot, because of its sheer volume, be included in the history books. The daily acquisition processes still continue and the British Library receives issues of the newspapers published in the British Isles.

Some new titles may require a little more effort from the staff to ensure their safe arrival; not all publishers are like Mr E B Giles of the *Yarmouth Free Lance* who wrote the following postcard to the British Museum's copyright agent Mr Lethbridge:

Free Lance Office, 1 April 1871
"I have sent papers regular. Just managed with an accident, hurt my eye severely, cannot attend at present to your required papers mentioned, none in stock. If necessary must hunt around the town."
E B Giles [*Punctuation added*]

Perhaps the date is of significance, but the newspapers were never sent to London.

Modern technology is being introduced to control the influx of newspapers and their eventual exploitation. Microfilm is used as a substitute for frail or damaged volumes, whilst up-to-date conservation methods are applied to volumes with high intrinsic value. The newspaper is ephemeral, designed to be read and possibly kept until the next issue appears. The newspapers held in the British Library's safekeeping are rarities; most of their fleeting companions will have long since disappeared – thrown away, used as kindling or wrappings for rubbish.

• *The Suffragette,"* October 18, 1912.

THE SUFFRAGETTE

Edited by CHRISTABEL PANKHURST, LL.B.

VOL. I.—No. 1. FRIDAY, OCTOBER 18, 1912. Price 1d. Weekly (Post Free, 1½d.)

"If this Session is to end without a measure of Votes for Women passing the House of Commons, then the sooner the Liberal-Labour-Nationalist Coalition is overthrown, and this Parliament dissolved, the better."—*W.S.P.U. Election Policy*, p. 7.

FOREWORD.

"The Suffragette," of which this is the first issue, is the Official Organ of the Women's Social and Political Union, the militant organisation for obtaining Votes for Women. The name Suffragette, first applied to members of the W.S.P.U. by the Newspapers, has, by use and association, been purified of any opprobrium or distasteful significance it may have borne in the past. It is now a name of highest honour, and women in ever-increasing thousands bear it with pride; and until a better is invented it stands as no other word does for the independence, courage, public spirit, and, we may add, humour, which are the attributes of the really womanly woman. The Suffragettes are women who have profited by the freedom won for them by the pioneers of the movement. They are the advance-guard of the new womanhood. The Suffragette has come to stay! That is why we have called this paper by her name.

BIGGEST FREE GIFT YET!

WOMAN'S OWN

No. 1
... 15
1932

2d.

3 Skeins OF WOOL INSIDE

TO EVERY READER

THE DANDY COMIC

No1 DEC 4 · 1937 EVERY FRIDAY 2D

KORKY THE CAT

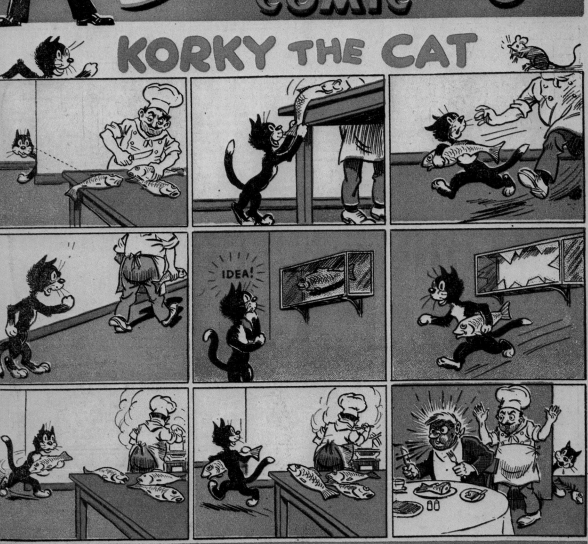

Nº1 EXPRESS WHISTLER FREE INSIDE

Amongst these crumbling newspapers the reader is able to discover early attempts at matchmaking in the pages of the *Matrimonial Post*, aimed mainly at women looking for husbands (3). It is open to conjecture how today's modern woman would accept such a publication. *The Suffragette* recalls the struggle undergone by British women before they were allowed to elect their Parliamentary representatives (4). *Woman's Own* has provided entertainment and interest since 1932, and is a valuable record of social change (5).

Amusing interludes are provided by *Comic Cuts*, published by Lord Northcliffe in the late 1890s and early 1900s, and the pioneer of a whole range of comic papers (7). It was succeeded in 1937 by *The Dandy* and *The Beano* (first published in 1938), both of which have proved so popular that they continue to be published.

Two particular rarities in the Library's collections provide interesting perspectives on episodes in the history of the United States. The single issue of *Buffalo Bill's Wild West Courier*, published on 7 May 1892 for the Earl's Court exhibition, gave Londoners a taste of the Wild West, and fuelled hero-worship of Colonel Cody. The *Daily Citizen* of 2 July 1863 is much closer to an historical event; for it was prepared by a Confederate printer but finished off by victorious Union soldiers after their entry into Vicksburg. The siege had taken its toll on paper supplies, and the single sheet newspaper had to be printed on pages from a wallpaper sample book (9).

Since the 17th century, newspapers have recorded (and often distorted) the momentous occasions in history. The early days of the Russian Revolution, for example, can be relived through the pages of *Pravda* (11). Bold, clear design – in the manner of a poster – proclaims the rise of Lenin. An earlier revolution, enacted in the chamber of the Assemblée Nationale, is similarly recorded. The rare *Affiches de la Commune*, from the Paris of 1793, were designed as wall posters and printed on poor quality rag paper (which yet survives much better than modern newsprint); they enable us to come close to the experience of the Parisians themselves, anxious for news as the 'reign of terror' is inaugurated.

Newspapers have been printed on many materials other than paper. Silk or satin, for example, were used to print newspapers in limited numbers for special occasions – such as a Royal marriage or visit. These might be produced for civic dignitaries and the newspaper proprietors themselves, and naturally were forwarded to the Royal personages involved (although it appears that none have found their way into the Royal archives or to the British Library). The practice continues; in 1985 Her Majesty the Queen was

7 Lord Northcliffe introduced *Comic Cuts* in 1890 to project *Answers* whose circulation was not robust enough in its early months. *Comic Cuts* was intended for both young and old readers, combining illustrations with text. (*Comic Cuts*, 16 July 1910.)

"COMIC CUTS." No. ½

NO. 6 OF "THE LONDON LIBRARY" CONTAINS 'SHADOWS of LONDON.' 1D. Everywhere.

Comic Cuts.

One Hundred Laughs for a Halfpenny.

1D. ½

PRICE ONE HALFPENNY.

No. 1,053. [Registered.]

JULY 16, 1910.

Catching the Post.
(See below.)

THE BURGLING SEASON FALLS FLAT AT MULBERRY FLATS.

1. The London burgling season commenced last week in the fashionable residential quarter that our Flats have made so famous. For many days there had been burglaries, and rumours of burglaries, in the neighbourhood, and the Flatites had grown so nervous that, with the exception of Oofbird, Esq., they refused to go to bed at the usual time. Miss Oldmaid dozed in her armchair, Mr. Bachelorboy sat up writing poetry to the girl at his favourite bun-shop, whilst Frowsy Freddie kept a sharp look-out at the attic window. "Hallo! what's up?" mused Freddie, when he saw two suspicious-looking loiterers place a dummy pillar-box over Oofbird's coal-hole and disappear inside.

2. There's no mistake about it, those Bloomsbury burglars were an artful pair of dodgers, but not quite as artful as our attic aristocrat. Oh, dear, no! You've got to get up very early in the morning to catch Frowsy Fred on the hop. While Christopher Crowbar was making merry with Oofbird's safe, and Dartmoor Dick was playing at touch wood and whistle with Mr. Bachelorboy and his roll-top desk, Frowsy was getting very busy with a clothes'-line and a meat-hook. "I'm glad to see that somebody manages to get a bit of sleep these nights," murmured Freddie, as he deftly manœuvred the hook into the letter slot, while the tired constable dreamed of promotion.

3. Directly the pillar-box began to wobble a little Frowsy knew that the bold, bad burg-u-lars were making their exit through the coal-hole, and he thereupon gave the rope a mighty jerk, with the happy result depicted above. "It's funny how suddenly to the pleasant realities of life. "I shall be promoted, after all!" And he was so pleased to see burglar number one, that he fell upon the poor fellow's neck and nearly smothered him out of sheer joy. Then the giddy Flatites all shouted "Police!" at once, and the Bloomsbury crib-crackers were duly arrested and lodged in a Government hotel.

Speech bubbles: "WAKE UP AUNTIE!" "NEXT COLLECTION I AM HERE." "GOOD GRASHUS! PROMOTION IS MINE!" "POLICE!" "SNAG"

SOUND ARGUMENT.

Sergeant: "Why didn't you get up when you heard the bugle sound?"
Recruit: "I didn't know the tune!"

MADE TO FIT ITS OWNER.

1. "Great Christopher Wren! What a funny-looking door! Now, why was it ever built in that strange shape?" pondered the tourist.

2. And just then the door opened, and the owner of the house stepped out, and the tourist saw the explanation staring him in the face.

LOOK AT THE CATERPILLAR!

Clara: "Oh, there's dear George! He's crept up behind me to surprise me, but I can feel his dear moustache!"

8 *below.* Buffalo Bill's Wild West Show delighted crowds in London in 1887 and 1892. Very few of the 100,000 copies of this free exhibition newspaper have survived. (*Buffalo Bill's Wild West Courier and International Horticultural Exhibition Gazette*, 7 May 1892.)

International Horticultural Exhibition Ga

..isher.] **EARL'S COURT, LONDON, SATURDAY, MAY 7th, 189**

"Col. Cody has done his part in bringing America and England nearer together."— Editorial, London *Times*, November 1st, 1887.

ERANS.

OF '87.

LL'S

T

RT. '92.

E,

VELL,

PAIGN

NTS.

STUDY,

L

BITION.

R CAMP,

ROSES.

ena and Camp
ng buildings,
ardens, Main
he Flowers of
nanner of the
International
Buffalo Bill's
Mecca of the
of '92. The
velty, and the
'87—Jubilee
enterprise, in
to be familiar
ame Original
o, Col. W. F.

Cody and
magnitud
former o
POSITIVEL
American
POSITIVE
of passing
more com
fates have
will be in
various T
since the
uprising
and the p
covered
journal
which pl
first new
Wild W
every ex
an unex
originalit
many tho
uprising
causes b
Bull," an
the amus
most crit
authentic
landing, t
without
the side o
the loss o
going alo
a the re
Miles. H
fulfilment
resulting
the kindl
exploited
after the
Mission,
than was
acknowle
in the vi
natural e
triumpha
a larger
"Short
twenty-th
by the a
many of
all partic
in the blo
in Ameri
the world
object of
realistic,
than any
and histo

COLONEL W. F. CODY—"BUFFALO BILL."
"Be sure you're right, then go ahead."—*Davy Crockett.*

THE DAILY CITIZEN.

J. M. SWORDS. .... Proprietor

VICKSBURG, MISS.

THURSDAY, JULY 2, 1863.

☞ Mrs. Cisco was instantly killed on Monday, on Jackson road. Mrs. Cisco's husband is now in Virginia, a member of Moody's artillery, and the death of such a loving, affectionate and dutiful wife will be a loss to him irreparable.

☞ We are indebted to Major Gillespie for a steak of Confederate beef *alias* meat. We have tried it, and can assure our friends that if it is rendered necessary, they need have no scruples at eating the meat. It is sweet, savory and tender, and so long as we have a mule left we are satisfied our soldiers will be content to subsist on it.

☞ Jerro Askew, one of our most esteemed merchant citizens, was wounded at the works in the rear of our city a few days since, and breathed his last on Monday. Mr. Askew was a young man of strict integrity, great industry and an honor to his family and friends. He was a member of Cowan's artillery and by the strict discharge of his duties and his obliging disposition, won the confidence and esteem of his entire command. May the blow his family have sustained be mitigated by Him who doeth all things well.

☞ Grant's forces did a little firing on Tuesday afternoon, but the balance of that day was comparatively quiet. Yesterday morning they were very still, and continued so until early in the afternoon, when they sprung a mine on the left of our centre, and opened fire along the line for some distance. We have not been able to ascertain anything definitely as to our loss, but as our officers were on the lookout for this move of the enemy, the expectations of the Yankees were not realized by a great deal.

☞ Among many good deeds we hear spoken of with pride by our citizens, we cannot refrain from mentioning the case of Mr. F. Kiser. This gentleman, having more corn than he thought was necessary to last him during the siege of this place, portioned off what would do him for the brief interval that will ensue before the arrival of succor to our garrison, and since that time has relieved the wants of many families *free of charge!* May he live long and prosper,

9 A rare issue of the *Daily Citizen*, produced in Vicksburg during the American Civil War. It was printed on wallpaper as no newsprint was available. (*Daily Citizen*, 2 July 1863.)

N°. 144.

AFFICHES
DE
LA COMMUNE DE PARIS.

Du 27 du 2me mois, l'an 2me de la République Françaiſe, une & indiviſible.

Séance du 26 Brumaire de la deuxième année de la République une & indiviſible.

LA ſection des Marchés ſe préſente en maſſe; elle déclare qu'à l'exemple des magiſtrats du peuple, elle marche ſur ſes traces, en abjurant toutes les erreurs & le menſonge des miniſtres du culte catholique, & qu'elle ne reconnoît maintenant d'autre divinité que la liberté & l'égalité, & d'autre guide que la raiſon.

La citoyenne Vantin, de la même ſection, dépoſe deux médailles, l'une eſt ſa pièce de mariage, portant l'effigie de nos tyrans. Le citoyen Rouſſelet dépoſe une médaille en argent, portant des ſignes de féodalité. Le conſeil arrête qu'il ſera donné acte à l'une & à l'autre de la remiſe de ces pièces, & la mention au procès-verbal.

Sur les obſervations des citoyens de la ſection des Marchés, le Conſeil-Général arrête que les vétérans porteront un plumet aux trois couleurs; au lieu du plumet blanc, & qu'ils n'auront plus ni écharpes ni ceintures; que le préſent ſera envoyé au commandant-général, avec invitation de le faire exécuter, & injonction au commandant du bataillon des vétérans de s'y conformer.

Le Conſeil arrête pareillement, ſur la demande de la ſection des Marchés, que la croix qui eſt au-deſſus du poteau de la place des Marchés ſera enlevée. Renvoyé au département des travaux publics.

Le citoyen Pallory, excellent patriote, bleſſé dans une fête civique, & dénué des moyens de ſubſiſter, réclame les ſecours du Conſeil. Le Conſeil arrête qu'il ſera accordé audit citoyen un ſecours proviſoire de cinquante livres, pris ſur les fonds que le ſecrétaire-greffier peut avoir entre ſes mains.

Une députation des ci-devant frères de la Charité, remettent au Conſeil les joujoux qui ont ſervi depuis tant de ſiècles d'armes aux fanatiques, & avec leſquels ils aveugloient le peuple dans le temple de l'ignorance. Le Conſeil-Général arrête que ces objets d'argenterie & de vermeil ſeront envoyés au comité révolutionnaire de la ſection de l'Unité, avec injonction de faire ſon devoir.

Le Conſeil-Général arrête qu'à l'avenir le Conſeil ne recevra aucune lettre de prêtriſe, mais que les citoyens qui viendront faire de pareils dépôts ſe retireront au ſecrétariat, pour faire enregiſtrer leur déclaration.

Le procureur de la Commune expoſe aux yeux du Conſeil un drapeau rouge, trouvé par le concierge dans un grenier; il demande quel emploi le Conſeil veut faire de la plus belle étoffe. Le conſeil arrête, après pluſieurs débats, que le drapeau ſeroit envoyé à la commiſſion centrale de bienfaiſance, pour être vendu au profit des pauvres.

Le Conſeil autoriſe le comité révolutionnaire de la ſection de l'Indiviſibilité à inviter les citoyens membres du diſtrict de Meaux à rendre la liberté, ainſi que les deux ſeptiers d'avoine, au citoyen Aimard, loueur de carroſſes, rue des Tournelles, & au citoyen Thiébaut, leſquels ont été arrêtés à Chelles, pour avoir acheté de l'avoine audit lieu, avec un bon du comité révolutionnaire, qui reconnoît ces deux individus pour de bons citoyens.

La ſection en maſſe de la Fraternité déclare qu'elle a renvoyé tous ſes prêtres & fermé l'égliſe de ſon arrondiſſement. Le Conſeil en arrête la mention civique au procès-verbal & l'inſertion aux affiches.

La Commune de la Montagne de Bel-Air (Saint-Germain-en-Laye) renvoie à la Commune de Paris la citoyenne Morin, dont le paſſe-port n'étoit pas en règle. Renvoyé à l'adminiſtration de police.

Un membre de la commiſſion du Temple fait un rapport ſur les dépenſes de cette maiſon de détention. Le procureur de la Commune ſe récrie ſur les dépenſes énormes qu'occaſionnent ces détenus. Le Conſeil arrête qu'il ſe tranſportera en maſſe à la Convention, pour demander que les priſonniers du Temple ſoient renvoyés dans les priſons ordinaires, & traités comme tous les autres détenus, & que ces individus ſoient jugés dans le plus court délai.

Le procureur de la Commune déclare au Conſeil qu'il a pris ſur Gagnant des renſeignemens qui ſont tous à ſon avantage; il croit devoir lui rendre cette juſtice, & ſe rétracter ſur ſon compte; il penſe qu'il doit être reporté à l'adminiſtration de police. Le Conſeil adhère à la demande du procureur de la Commune & rétablit Gagnant dans la place d'adminiſtrateur de police.

La ſection des Quinze-Vingts apporte les objets de Charlataniſme des prêtres, & entre autre la fameuſe chemiſe de Saint-Louis, qui n'eſt qu'une chemiſe de femme. Le Conſeil arrête qu'elle ſera brûlée en plein Conſeil, ce qui eſt ſur-le-champ exécuté; quant aux autres objets, le Conſeil arrête qu'ils ſeront envoyés à la monnoie, & les autres à la fonderie de l'Arſenal.

Le citoyen Jeannequin, employé aux travaux militaires de l'Arſenal, fait dépoſer par ſon neveu, une épée qu'il a priſe en combattant l'ennemi à l'armée des Alpes; il y joint un écu de 6 liv. à l'effigie du tyran. Le Conſeil reçoit cette offre & en arrête la mention civique au procès-verbal.

Les canonniers de Paris conſentent à faire chaque jour le ſervice, plutôt que de permettre à des citoyens ſuſpects de remplacer leurs camarades qui ſont partis avec l'armée révolutionnaire; ils demandent qu'il ne ſoit formé aucune nouvelle compagnie dans les ſections.

Le procureur de la Commune prend de-là occaſion pour parler contre l'eſprit du corps;

miſſion priſe dans le ſein des ſociétés populaires, qui ſera chargée de recevoir ces dépouilles du fanatiſme expirant, & d'en donner quittance.

V. Le nombre & la qualité de tous les objets livrés ſeront imprimés & affichés dans toutes les Communes.

VI. Les miniſtres des cultes qui, par l'acte ſublime du mariage & par le concours de leurs lumières, briſeront le bandeau de l'erreur, apprendront au peuple la ſainte vérité & tâcheront de réparer les maux affreux que l'hypocriſie de leurs prédéceſſeurs a vomi ſur la ſurface de la terre, ſeront regardés comme les apôtres de l'humanité, & recommandés à la

Hauteur de la rivière. — Le 27 du deuxième mois, 3 pieds

DE L'IMPRIMERIE DES AFFICH

Россійская Соціалъ-Демократическая Рабочая Партія

Пролетаріи всѣхъ странъ, соединяйтесь!

ПРАВДА

ОРГАНЪ
Центральнаго Комитета
и
Петербургскаго Комитета
Р. С.-Д. Р. П.

Суббота, 23-го Іюня (10 Іюня ст. ст.) 1917 г. ЕЖЕДНЕВНАЯ ГАЗЕТА. Цѣна № 8 коп. № 78.

Ко всѣмъ трудящимся, ко всѣмъ рабочимъ и солдатамъ Петрограда.

Въ виду того, что Съѣздъ Совѣтовъ Рабочихъ и Солдатскихъ Депутатовъ, къ которому присоединился Исполнительный Комитетъ Совѣта Крестьянскихъ Депут., постановилъ,

признавши обстоятельства совершенно исключительными, запретить всякія, даже мирныя, демонстраціи на три дня,

Центр. Комитетъ Росс. С.-Д. Рабочей Партіи

ПОСТАНОВЛЯЕТЪ

ОТМѢНИТЬ назначенную имъ на 2 часа дня, въ субботу, демонстрацію.

Центральный Комитетъ призываетъ всѣхъ членовъ партіи и всѣхъ сочувствующихъ ей провести это постановленіе въ жизнь.

presented with a special issue of *The Times*, on the occasion of the paper's bicentenary. Occasionally coloured portraits (1, 2) or other pictures were printed as inserts in a magazine, for promotional purposes, and these might then be framed by collectors.

It is not unknown for newspapers to have been forged. *The Times* seems to have suffered more than most from such imitation. One silk issue, recounting Wellington's victory at Waterloo in 1815, was discovered in Australia – and there are several other examples. If this is the sincerest form of flattery, then the forgers might have taken the trouble to use the correct format and typeface! The Nazi propaganda ministry had more sinister motives when it prepared a forged issue (with incorrect typeface) of the *Evening Standard*, dated 17 February 1940, for aerial distribution over London. There is no evidence that copies were ever dropped over the capital – and, judging by the unintentional humour of some of the advertisements, it is an open question whether any Londoner would have been taken in by the forgery – although it is possible that the consignment was released over Portsmouth.

Hereafter ensue the trewe encountre or
Bataple lately don betwene .Englãde and.
Scotlande. In whiche bataple the .Scottis=
he .Kynge was slayne.

The maner of thaduaũcesynge of my lord of
Surrey tresourier and .Marshall of .Englande
and leuetenãte generall of the north pties of th
e same with .xxvi .M. men towardes the kyn=
ge of .Scottz and his .Armye vewed and nõ/
bred to an/hundred thousande men at/theleest.

Early days: the 17th and 18th centuries

The history of newspapers in England could be said to begin around 1513, when a news pamphlet giving an eye-witness account of the battle of Flodden was published. It had lists of casualties and a report on the Englishmen who had distinguished themselves in the field, and was illustrated with a charming woodcut (12). This is the first account of any historical event to be printed in England, and as such has been called 'the foundation stone of the history of English journalism'. It is also a nearly unique survival; apart from a few other printed reports (concerning the Armada, in 1588, for example), there were no similar pamphlets produced for another 100 years.

The English newspaper developed gradually. Before the printed page became readily available, the ordinary person relied upon ballad singers or the town-crier for his news. Many country people would never have travelled more than twenty miles from their villages, and news from London or other great places would have held a fascination for them.

12 The first illustrated English news pamphlet was the *True Encounter* containing a contemporary account of the battle of Flodden in 1513. *True Encounter. Hereafter ensure the true encounter and batayle lately don betwene Englãd and Scotlande, etc.* Emprynted by me. Richarde. Faques [1513(?)]. [C.123 d.33.]

The aristocracy would have been able to afford subscriptions to manuscript newsletters, but they were expensive and slow to produce. The methods used were those practised by medieval monks and scribes. Foreign or domestic letters were received at the offices of gentlemen such as Henry Muddiman or Ichabod Dawks, where teams of copyists would translate and reproduce their contents. For these newsletters, subscribers could be charged comparatively large amounts by today's reckoning – up to £5 or more – which automatically meant that their circulation was limited to the wealthy (13).

Printing had previously been confined to books which were subject to religious or State control. Before 'newspapers' appeared, publishers provided an eager and often gullible public with broadsides which carried 'news'. The unsophisticated, largely illiterate populace was easily satisfied with tracts of a religious nature, or those which described disasters such as fires or floods, often attributed to the wrath of God. This type of publication continued to appear even after the first English newspapers were sold in London in the early decades of the 17th century.

The British Library has a number of these early broad-sheets. Usually they were illustrated with woodcuts; the agricultural worker who could not read might be more inclined to believe that the article were true if his literate neighbour assured him that the illustration depicted the events spoken about. In many ways this was a continuation of the medieval concept of decorating churches with colourful scenes from the Scriptures to educate an illiterate but faithful congregation.

DAWKS's News-Letter.

Sʳ London

August 3. 699.

Last night we received an Holland Mail, with some of these particulars following.

Lemberg, July 22. The Baſſa Capigi, Treaſurer General to the Grand Seignior, arrived at Camineck on the 6th. inſtant, and gave Orders to the Governour to prepare to March out with his Garriſon, and evacuate that Fortreſs to the Poles; whereupon the Turks have already begun to pack up their Baggage. The Hoſpodar of Walachia is alſo arrived upon the Frontiers, and is laying a Bridge over the Dnieſter, for the more convenient carrying of the Baggage. The Field Marſhal of the Crown has ſent to acquaint the King herewith.

Warſaw, July 28. The Diet is now like to have a good Iſſue, the King having Declared that he will maintain the Liberties of the People; that his Saxon Troops were all on their March homewards; That he will keep no Regiments by his Perſon, but only a Guard of 1200 Men at his own Charge, all of them Poles and Lithuanians: That if the Saxons do not March out of the Kingdom within the time limited, or return again on any Pretence whatſoever, without conſent of the Republick, it ſhall be lawful for the Nobility to Aſſemble on Horſeback without his Order, and Treat them as Publick Enemies. And in return hereof the Diet have obliged themſelves to ſecure his Majeſties Perſon with their utmoſt Power; that they will Severely Puniſh all that Act or but Speak againſt him: That all Libels againſt him ſhall be Burnt by the Hand of the Hangman; and the Authors of them ſerv'd in the ſame manner, if they can be apprehended. His Majeſty will hold a Diet in Saxony in September; and its ſaid he will bring his Queen hither with him when he returns.

Hamburg, Auguſt 4. Dr. Meyer, the Miniſter having Printed his Latin Oration upon the Marriage of the King of the Romans, on Cloth of Silver and Gold, and edg'd every Leaf it with Point of Venice, which altogether coſt this City 500 Crowns, he ſent the ſame to the Emperour and King of the Romans, who have thereupon made the Doctor a Palſgrave, and given him his Patent free.

Hague, Auguſt 8. They write from Nieuenheuſen in the County of Benthem, that 300 Neuburgers came to put the Countrey under Military Execution, for not ſubmitting to the Popiſh Count; but that a Body of Dutch Soldiers advancing, who were ſent by the States to ſupport the Proteſtant Count, put the Neuburgers to flight, having kill'd a Lieutenant and wounded three others. Letters from Hungary ſay, that General Nehm, who was impower'd to be preſent at adjuſting the Frontiers, falling into ſome Difference with the Baſſa of Temeſwaer, Struck him Dead from his Horſe; whereupon ſome other Turkiſh Officers taking up the Quarrel, there were 30 or 40 Men Killed on both ſides; however the Commiſſioners went on with adjuſting the Frontiers. Admiral

One such illustrated work which conveyed the news of particular events and satirised the folly of the time is *A True Report of certaine wonderfull overflowings of Waters now lately in Summersetshire, Norfolk, and other places in England, destroying many thousands of men* . . . printed by W.I. for E. White London: [1607] (**14**). The sermonising tone reflects the author's self-appointed task of relating natural disasters to a call for repentance. This type of tract usually moved along at a rapid pace to sustain the reader's interest.

Broad-sheets often gave accounts of supernatural visions. A common image was that of a figure which appeared in the sky, usually at the scene of a battle or siege, especially if the forces of Christendom were fighting the 'Turk'. Writers sometimes stretched the credulity of their readers to great lengths.

The first English-language newspapers which are recognisably newspapers (that is, folded news-sheets) were published in Holland. The earliest ones have no title as such, but simply start with an opening sentence. Like the tracts they were published at irregular intervals. George Veseler, an Amsterdam publisher, could be called the earliest 'newspaper' editor. His 'corantos' or news-books of 1620 and 1621 brought the news of central Europe to London and beyond. Typical titles are *Corante, or Newes, from Italy* . . . *etc.* (**15**).

Censorship was immediately imposed on the news which came in from abroad, especially where it was judged detrimental to the King or Ministers of State. The truth as it was seen had to be kept from the common people because they had to be prevented from discussing matters of State which did not concern them. The events of the Thirty Years War (1618–1648) however, became as well-known in Britain as they were on the continent of Europe, despite official attempts at increased censorship.

The first Englishman to publish a regular newsbook in England was Thomas Archer of Cornhill, London, in 1620. He was followed by Nicholas Bourne and Nathaniel Butler, who eventually entered into partnership to supply London with news, until the outbreak of the Civil War. As long as they did not add to or change the news translated from the Dutch corantos which were their source, their printing licence was not revoked by the Star Chamber. Others fared less happily. Archbishop Laud as censor of the press in the 1630s and 1640s carried out these duties with cruel tyranny. Offending printers were branded, or fined heavily, whipped through the streets or thrown into prison for expressing opinions contrary to the Archbishop's. The printers were to get their revenge when he fell from favour.

13 Subscribers paid 30*s* a quarter for *Dawks's Newsletter* whose appearance resembled manuscript newsletters. The beautiful type-face and scriveners' conventional heading and abbreviations contributed to the effect. (*Dawks's Newsletter*, 3 August [1]699.)

1607.

A true report of certaine wonderfull ouerflowings

of Waters, now lately in Summerset-shire, Norfolke, and other
places of England: destroying many thousands of men, women,
and children, ouerthrowing and bearing downe
whole townes and villages, and drowning
infinite numbers of sheepe and
other Cattle.

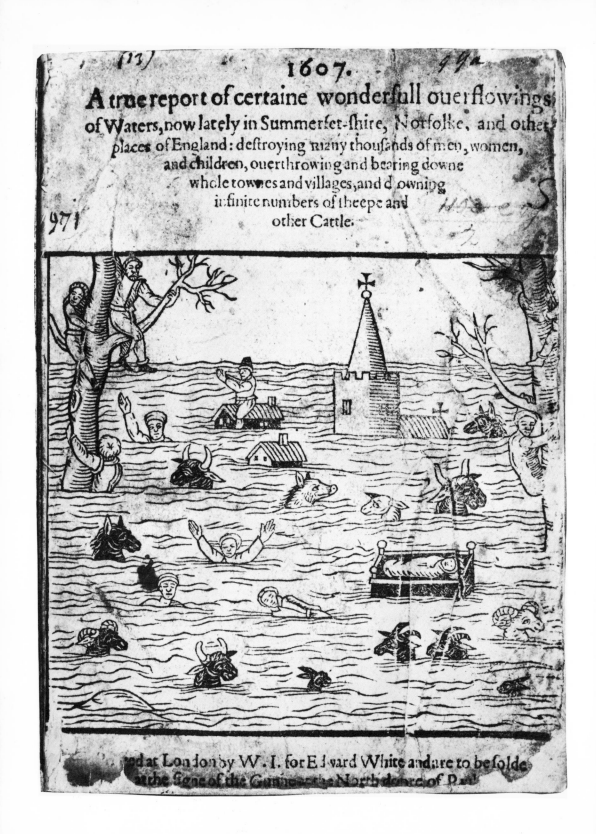

Printed at London by W. I. for Edward White and are to be solde
at the signe of the Gunne at the North doore of Paul

CORANTE, OR, NEVVES FROM
Italy, Germanie, Hungarie, Poland, Bohemia and France. 1621.

From Venice the 1. of Iuly 1621.

HEre the longer the more, preparation is made for warres.

There was a Commiſſion ſent to Naples, and from thence to be ſent to Millane, which is a bad token that Valtolina ſhall be reſtored.

It is written from Turnio, that the Duke thereof hath muſtred all his Horſe-men, and the greateſt part of his Foote-men at Miraflores, and hath ſent them to Cutri and Zenda, to what intent it is not knowne.

Letters from Genouo certifie that in the Sea by Corſica: There are 8. Turkiſh Shippes, that doe great hurt, and from Bergamo it is written, That the Prouediteur Contarini hath ſent men into Martinengo, whether meſt of the Commaunders, beſides 6000. Foot and 2000. Horſemen are already come, it is thought they will fortifie Romano, or ſome other places vpon the frontiers.

To Millane there are 500. crownes come by Letters of Exchange, and there are 4. Companies of Souldiers ſent to Valtelnia,

The Duke of Sauoy hath committed the gouernment wholly to his ſonne, and onely reſerued the ordering of the warres vnto himſelfe.

From Vianna the 29 of Iune 1621.

The 18. of this moneth, this Emperours Maieſtie with a great houſhold trayne rod to Sel, and in the morning betimes, before hee departed, the Denmarke Ambaſſadors tooke their leaues, and went from hence, but haue done nothing in the Palſgraues behalfe.

The Generall Bucquoy lyeth ſtill before Newheuſel, and makes ſtrong ſconces about it: Thoſe of Diepenbach haue cut downe the Milles, and thoſe that are beſieged expect 8000. men to relieue them, they iſſue out dayly. Bethlem Gabor is yet at Caſcow, ſtaying for the Turkiſh helpe.

The Earle of Colalde is yet with his Army at Regnitz vpon the Budzaners Country There is Hongarian helpe come vnto them, and thereby they encountred together, and fought, in which fight there are many on both ſides ſlaine, the certainety whereof is dayly expected.

The 19. of this moneth, the Lord Helmbert Georg, was carried priſoner from hence, to the Duke of Bauaria, and there are alſo 9 perſons of good quality choſen here out of 16. men to be examined, and are committed priſoners.

The newes continueth, that the Marquis of Iagerſdorp hath the Princely Caſtle of Neuſz, and hath taken the three Princely Officers and the Counſell into his ſecurity, that there are men taken vp openly in Neuſz for Bethlem Gabor, and there is a thouſand Ritters, and 1000. Muskatieres already entertained, and that the Colonell Lobuyſen hath brought 30 thouſand Duckets from Bethlem to Neuſz, to take vp more Souldiers.

From Vianna the 30 of Iune 1621.

From Comorra Letters of the 19. certifie, that Bucquoy, Maximilian van Lichtenſteyn, and the Lord Diepenbach, with 40. Horſemen went out of the Campe before Newheuſel, and were by the Hoongarians that lay in the Woods ſet vpon and encloſed on all ſides, ſo that none of them could eſcape away but hee was taken, ſo that of them there is 18 of the principalleſt perſons ſlaine, and thoſe in Newheuſel doe great hurt vnto our ſide.

From Prague the 29 of Iune 1620.

After the Emperours Commiſſioners had examined the priſoners here, this rigorous ſentence was pronounced againſt them, and ſent vnto the Emperor.

1. WIlliam Poppel of Lobkowitz condemned to forfait life, honour, and goods, and to be beheaded, but by grace ſhewed him by the Emperour, he is condemned to perpetuall impriſonment. *Chiefe Landhoof Maſter.*

2 Paul Ritſchen condemned as before, but fauoured alſo as before. *Chiefe Chanceler*

3 Ioachim Andreas Schlick condemned to haue his right hand cut off, to be quartered, and his quarters hanged in foure places in the Streetes, his head to be ſet vpon the Bridge Tower, but grace being ſhewed him, hee is to haue his right hand and his head cut off, and ſet vpon the Tower. *Burggraue of Carlc-ſteyn.*

4 Wentzel van Budowith condemned to haue his right hand, and his head to be cut off, and quartered, his quarters to hang in the Streetes, but grace being ſhewed him, he is to haue his head cut off, and ſet vpon the Tower, and his goods confiſcate.

5 Chriſtopher Harrand condemned to loſe his life and goods, and to be beheaded. *Preſident of the Bohemian Chamber.*

6 Caſper Caplar, a man of 80 yeeres old, condemned to loſe life and good, to haue his head cut off, and his body quartered, but grace being giuen him, hee muſt only haue his head cut off, and ſet vpon the Tower. *Chiefe Secretary of the land.*

7 Procop Dobrowſetzky, condemned to loſe life and goods, to haue his head cut off, and ſet on the Tower, *Vnder Chamber-laine.*

8 Bohuſlaw Michalowitzſch, to forſait life & goods, with the Sword to haue his head cut off, and his body quartered: but grace offered his head onely to be cut off, and ſet on the Tower. *Old Burgraue of Carleſtone*

9 Frederick Buchlaw, to haue his head cut off, his body quartered, and to be hanged in the Streetes, but grace offered him, he is to haue his head onely cut off, and ſet on the Tower, and his goods confiſcate.

10 Otto van Loſs, quartered aliue, and his body hanged vp, his head ſet on the Tower, but grace ſhewed, his head only is to be cut off, and ſet vpon the Tower, and his goods confiſcate.

11 Hans Weſtrowitz, to bee executed with the Sword, and his goods confiſcate, but grace offered, hee is condemned to perpetuall impriſonment.

12 Felix Wentzel, Pieto Petzſchky, body and goods loſt, to be beheaded, but grace offered, the execution is ſuſpended.

13 Dioniſius Eſcherin, Caſtle Hoffman body and goods forſaited, his two firſt fingers and his head to be cut off, and caſt downe into the Caſtle ditch, but grace offered, his head ſhal be cut off, & his goods confiſcate.

14 Wolfgang Haſlawer ſent to Raab in the frontier houſe.

15 Wilhelm Coningh Cluuisly life and goods loſt, to haue his head cut off, but his wife ſhall haue the goods that ſhe brought reſtored vnto her.

16 Valentin Cochan goods forſaited, his head cut off, and ſet on the Tower.

17 Theodorus Sixts goods forſaited, but he is to remaine in priſon.

18 Tobias Steffegh, to haue his head cut off, and ſet on the Tower, his goods confiſcate.

19 Chriſtoph Kober as aforeſaid.

20 Iohan Schultheitz van Katzenbergh, beheaded, and ſet vpon the Tower, his goods confiſcate.

21 Maxmiliaen Hoſhalig primas van Satz, as aforeſaid.

22 Iohn Ieſſenius Doctor his tongue cut out, quartered aliue, but grace giuen him, he is firſt to haue his

16 An unusual feature of this issue of the parliamentarian *Mercurius Civicus* was the inclusion of two portraits of King Charles I and Queen Henrietta Maria. The verse at the head of the page gave the reader an indication of the contents. (*Mercurius Civicus* no 8, 13/20 July 1643.)

The English Civil War

After the abolition of the Star Chamber in 1641, the press was freed and the contents of newsbooks enlivened. The style, adopted from the continental newsbooks, was improved; the beginnings of a recognisable journalistic 'technique', including feature articles and banner headlines, were adopted. By 1643 more titles had appeared. Londoners were fortunate in that they could choose from a dozen weekly newsbooks. A confusing array of similar titles flourished. *Diurnalls* and the Mercuries (Mercurius) opposed each other. The Royalist cause was supported by *Mercurius Aulicus* published at Oxford by Sir John Birkenhead, who did not change his allegiance

throughout the war. The Parliamentarians published the *Mercurius Britanicus* under the editorship of Thomas Audley, assisted by Marchamont Nedham. The latter was not averse to changing his allegiance from Parliament to the King when the time was opportune. At the end of the war he was totally discredited.

Illustrated 'journalism' became more important. Portraits of the leaders of both sides were used. *Mercurius Civicus*, published in London to contradict false information, used wood-cuts of King Charles and Queen Henrietta Maria to illustrate the news (16). The execution of King Charles on 30 January 1649 was represented by wood-cuts in broad-sheets (but not in the newsbooks). When the rule of Cromwell was consolidated after the defeat of King Charles II at Worcester, the newspapers which had sprung up rapidly disappeared. A few remained despite Parliament's press laws. In 1663 after the Restoration, the government ordered a strict limit on the number of master-printers and presses in London. Parliamentary reports were banned.

Post-Restoration newspapers

Of newspapers published in the 17th Century, the *London Gazette*, which originated in 1665 as the *Oxford Gazette*, is still published today, although it no longer contains news. Another famous title, *Lloyd's List*, was first started in 1734. Edward Lloyd had previously published *Lloyd's News* in 1695 with the same purpose – to provide accurate information on shipping movements and cargoes. This ran to only 76 issues, before Lloyd thought it wise to discontinue publication, his printer having put in unauthorised information which was untrue. Lloyd's Coffee House was one of many which flourished in London at the turn of the 17th century.

The Printing Act of 1663 was not renewed in 1695 due to party political wrangling between the Whigs and Tories. The immediate result was that legally permissible newspapers sprang up which did not always support the government. Freedom of speech, so long suppressed by censorship, flourished, until 1712 when the first of many Stamp Acts were brought before Parliament. This legislation

17 Vociferous arguments against the newspaper tax were published at intervals until its abolition in 1855. (*Felix Farley's Bristol Journal*, 10 June 1815.)

Intended Tax upon Newspapers and Advertisements.

It is with considerable feelings of regret, that we inform our readers, that the exigencies of the times are such, that the Minister has felt himself obliged to resort to a further taxation upon these necessary and already highly taxed vehicles of information. The number of Newspapers published in Great Britain and Ireland amounts to about 200. They contribute at this time annually to the revenue no less a sum than £450,000 !!! Is there another profession in the kingdom, that produces such a contribution from its mere mental exertions ? It surely becomes the Minister to pause, before he strains the sinews of so important an engine as the public Press too rightly. Our readers must have observed, that it was Mr. Vansittart's first intention to have raised the sum he now wants, by taxing advertisements according to their length. Of the impolicy of this measure, which we hesitate not to say would have suppressed one-third of the Provincial Prints, he has been con-

permitted government control of the number of printed newspapers. The penny Stamp Tax had to be embossed on the sheets used for printing and the cost of the stamp had to be paid in advance, a cost passed on to the reader. More or less overnight 50 per cent of London's newspapers disappeared. The Stamp Tax was also applied to the provincial press and publishers had to send paper to the Stamp Office in London for embossing with the die allocated to that newspaper for the purpose. The delays sometimes caused to production added to the costs of publication.

Although the newspaper publishers suffered when the tax had been imposed initially, it did not inhibit the appearance of new titles. There was a steady increase in titles and by 1776, on the outbreak of war with the American colonies, the extra $\frac{1}{2}$d tax was imposed on no fewer than 53 London newspapers. Later, Britain's involvement in the ruinously expensive Napoleonic Wars was partially financed through extra taxation raised by increases in the Stamp Tax (17). Successive governments refused to repeal these laws until 1855 when *The Times* and other well-conducted newspapers agitated for their abolition. The government abolished the Stamp Tax but subjected the newspapers to 1d postal tax instead.

Despite the fact that the provincial press did not really come into its own until 1855, it would be untrue to say that London held a monopoly on the news. Large population centres such as Bristol,

18 Provincial newspapers were often illustrated with a view of the town or city in which they were published. (*Ipswich Journal, or, Weekly Mercury*, 15/22 April 1721.)

Bath, York and Newark had their own printing presses and newspapers. London-trained printers such as Thomas Aris, who founded *Aris's Birmingham Gazette* on 16 November 1741, took their trade to the provinces to escape a capital crowded with newspapers. One of the earliest to appear was the *Worcester Post-Man* in 1710, which is still published today as *Berrow's Worcester Journal*. Early presses had been set up in Scotland and Ireland but the Newspaper Library's collections do not include anything published in the 17th century, apart from one issue of the *Edinburgh Gazette* dated Munday [sic] 18/21 September 1699.

One Dublin title, *Pue's Irish Intelligence*, was lost, presumed destroyed in the bomb damage inflicted upon the Newspaper Library during the Second World War.

The files of early 18th-century newspapers are representative in many cases rather than comprehensive. There are instances where complete files have not been obtained. The Irish newspaper titles in the Newspaper Library collection, for example, are only really comprehensive from the middle of the 19th century, although cities such as Cork, Belfast and Dublin were early centres of newspaper publishing.

Provincial titles imitated London newspapers in their layout (18, 19). At the same time, their contents were liberally pirated – as copyright could not be enforced during the 18th century. The *London Gazette* was freely quoted, together with the bills of mortality and city news. Local news had secondary importance in the provincial press due to the printer's reluctance to offend local dignitaries. It was one thing to report a London robbery or compromising relationship with the names of the participants carefully expunged, but quite another to report violence inflicted on a poacher by the local squire's gamekeepers before he was brought before the squire in his capacity as a magistrate.

Throughout the first 80 years of the 18th century a journalist had been nothing more than a hack writer, although some newspapers such as the *Morning Herald* (1780–1869) and the *Morning Chronicle* (1770–1862) were attempts to raise the genre's reputation. Other publications such as the *Gentleman's Magazine*, which was first published in 1781, had exhibited the characteristics of a newspaper, but it appeared monthly. This contained literary or moral essays, as had both *The Tatler* and *The Spectator* before it. All three titles are still excellent sources for historians who are looking for contemporary information, or the details of births, marriages and deaths, and of course for literary historians.

The last 15 years of the 18th century coincided with the birth of possibly the best-known newspaper in the world, and events which were to lead to the establishment of modern journalism.

JULY, 3, 1769.

By their MAJESTIES Servants,
From the THEATRES ROYAL.

At the THEATRE in CANTERBURY,
This Evening will be presented a COMEDY,
CALLED

The WONDER;
OR,
A Woman keeps a Secret.

Don FELIX, Mr. PERRY;
GIBBY, Mr. YOUNGER;
Col. BRITTON, Mr. READE; Don LOPEZ, Mr. BROOKES; Don PEDRO, Mr. BARN-SHAW; FREDERICK, Mr. CORNELIUS; LISSARDO, Mr. BARRINGTON; ALGUA-ZILE, Mr. REDMAN.
ISABELLA, Miss HELME.
FLORA, Mrs. GLOVER; INIS, Mrs. BAR-RINGTON;
VIOLANTE, Miss WARD.

To which will be added a Musical Entertainment, called,

M I D A S.

With all the Machinery and Decorations.
MIDAS, Mr. BROOKES; PAN, Mr. PERRY; APOLLO, Mr. RICHARDS; SILENO, Mr. BARNSHAW; DAMÆTAS, Mr. READE; JUPITER, Mr. THOMPSON, DAPHNE, Mrs. GLOVER; NYSA, Miss ATKINSON; MYSIS, Mrs. BARRINGTON; JUNO, Miss RICHLEY.

☞ *A great Expence having attended the bringing out this Piece, for the Machinery, &c. Nothing under the Full Price can be taken.*

Boxes 2s. 6d.   Pit 2s.   Gallery 1s.
The Doors to be opened at 6, and to begin exactly at 7 o'clock.   VIVANT REX & REGINA.
No Persons can be admitted behind the Scenes, nor any Money returned after the Curtain is drawn up.
Tickets to be had at the Red Lion, the Coffee-House, the King's Head, the Fountain; and at Mr. Smith's General Printing-Office, in St. Andrew's.
Places for the Boxes to be taken at the THEATRE, where a Book will be kept open for that Purpose, every Day, from Ten till One.
The DAYS of Performing are on MONDAYS, WEDNESDAYS, and FRIDAYS, till further Notice.

19 The typographical style of this provincial theatrical advertisement was typical of its day. (*Kentish Weekly Post*, 26 June 1769.)

The 19th century: the emergence of professional journalism

The *Daily Universal Register* (later *The Times*) was first published on 1 January 1785 by John Walter I, a bankrupt coal merchant, who had taken up printing at the age of 45 to repay his creditors. The purchase of the patented Logographic Press was in itself a means of entering the printing trade. He had not succeeded in interesting enough clients in logography, with which he intended to revolutionise the printing world. The newspaper was conceived as another venture to keep his presses in operation when not enough printing commissions were around. The *Daily Universal Register* was also meant to be an example of the merits of the press, whilst simultaneously acting as an advertisement and review sheet for his own books.

Walter set up a foreign news service for *The Times* in 1805 which became so accurate that the newspaper was trusted for its contents even by government ministers. This was a bone of contention within some official circles. By 1830, under Thomas Barnes, *The Times* had established itself as the most powerful and well-conducted newspaper in the country. John Walter II had introduced steam printing in 1814 and with two presses capable of producing 1,000 copies of the newspaper every hour, *The Times*'s excellent reputation for rational reporting of foreign and home news, was spread even farther afield. As the century ran its course *The Times* experienced high and low points in its fortunes.

The standards set by *The Times* for accuracy and interest were emulated to a lesser or greater extent by the other newspapers of the period. The private news service was the envy of other editors until the advent of the undersea telegraph cables laid by the 'Great Eastern' rendered foreign news accessible to anyone who could pay the telegraph charges. *The Times*'s monopoly was broken and newspapers like the Liberal *Daily News* and Conservative *Daily Telegraph* could compete on equal terms for material.

By 1856, the year after the repeal of the Stamp Tax, 200 newspapers had sprung up mushroom-like throughout the British Isles. Local and foreign news could be brought to people who lived near to the large towns and cities. Some newspapers which had been published weekly or twice weekly now changed their frequency. The *Manchester Guardian* and *The Scotsman* became daily newspapers. Famous titles such as the *Sheffield Daily Telegraph* and the *Liverpool Daily Post* were founded at this time.

Not all of the newspapers launched in 1856 survived. In the West Midlands for example, the *Dudley Weekly Times* went through three changes of title in 1858 in a vain attempt to attract readers. Others, like the *Midland Counties Evening Express* founded in 1874, still survive today. Now the Wolverhampton *Express and Star*, this

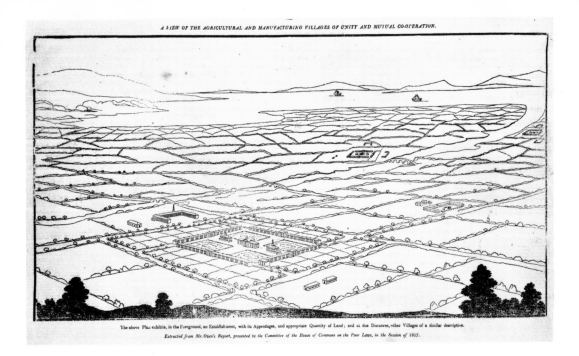

20 *right above*. It was unusual for *The Times* to grant so much space to a wood-block illustration in its early days. Robert Owen's attempts at socialist cooperation were fully described on a complete page. Later, as the newspaper became more influential, illustrations were dropped in favour of text. (*The Times*, 9 August 1817.)

newspaper enjoys an increasing circulation and healthy revenue.

With the abolition of paper tax in 1861 the way was opened for the development of presses fed by continuous reels of newsprint. As the demand for cheap newspapers increased, publishers became more aware of the rising costs of paper. The introduction of wood-pulp in the 1870s meant that newsprint could be manufactured more quickly and more cheaply.

Provincial journalists had developed their readers' awareness of local politics but sometimes the reporters found that they were not permitted to enter the local council chamber. Like their predecessors they had to combat petty censorship. Even if they managed to obtain access for their reporters, proprietors themselves were not permitted to become local justices or councillors for fear that they might be too closely associated with subsequently published reports. This position took a long time to alter but by the end of the 19th century some proprietors were JPs and even MPs. The wheel of respectability had finally turned full circle and the Grub Street hack of the 1750s was socially acceptable. Henry Labouchere, editor of *Truth* and Horatio Bottomley, editor of *John Bull*, are memorable names. Others were honoured with peerages or knighthoods. The Harmsworth brothers, Alfred and Harold, were created Lord Northcliffe and Lord Rothermere respectively. The practice continues today.

21 *right below*. Steam printing. Within a few months of its commencement, the *Illustrated London News* was using steam-driven printing machines to meet the demands of increasing circulation. (*Illustrated London News*, 2 Dec. 1843.)

22 *left below*. To cut costs newspaper publishers employed women at lower rates to fold and collate newspapers before automatic folding machines were invented.

23 *facing page*. The 'golden' issue of *The Sun* was published to celebrate Queen Victoria's coronation. In reality the gold was dusted bronze mixed with varnish. Gold inks did not become widely available until this century. (*The Sun*, 28 June 1838.)

The arrival of the two Harmsworth brothers in Fleet Street was to prove significant. Alfred Harmsworth had trained in all aspects of journalism and newspaper production. He was skilled at editing and layout. Harold had the ability to attract much needed advertising. These skills were a winning combination. Alfred founded a direct competitor to George Newnes's *Tit-Bits* when he published *Answers*. Another coup which the brothers achieved was the total reversal of the failing fortunes of the *Evening News*. This bankrupt newspaper had the highest circulation of all comparable London newspapers within three months of its acquisition by the Harmsworths in 1894.

Alfred Harmsworth, Lord Northcliffe, repeated this success with the *Daily Mail* which was launched on 4 February 1896. He knew the readership at which he was aiming. Echoing the success of women's illustrated magazines, a woman's page was featured in the *Daily Mail* together with light sporting columns. The news was rendered easy to read. Sub-editors had reduced each major story to its bare essentials but retained the basic facts. Northcliffe considered that the busy man or woman did not have time to wade through long columns of text to arrive at the crux of the story. It was this campaigning spirit which led him to acquire *The Times* in 1908 after protracted negotiations. He saved the newspaper from financial extinction and after introducing photographs to its pages and lighter articles he considered that he had brought *The Times* into the twentieth century.

00. An early folding machine by Harrild, *c.* 1879

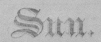

The Sun.

WITH WHICH THE "TRUE SUN" IS NOW INCORPORATED.

No. 14,289. LONDON, THURSDAY EVENING, JUNE 28, 1838. PRICE

God Save

Victoria R.

THE CORONATION.

Mr. Thompson, in his work on "The Processions and Ceremonies observed in the Coronation of the Kings and Queens of England," gives the following account of KING EDWARD'S CHAIR.

"This chair (commonly called "St. Edward's chair") is an ancient seat of solid, hard wood, with back and sides of the same, variously painted, in which the kings of Scotland were in former periods constantly crowned; but, having been brought out of the kingdom by King Edward I., in the year 1296, after he had totally overcome John Baliol king of Scots, it has ever since remained in the abbey of Westminster, and has been the royal chair in which the succeeding kings and queens of this realm have been inaugurated. It is in height 6 ft. 7 in., in breadth at the bottom, 38 in., and in depth 24 in.; from the seat to the bottom is 25 in., the breadth of the seat within the sides is 28 in., and the depth 18 in. At 9 inches from the ground is a board, supported at the four corners by as many lions. Between the seat and this board is enclosed a stone, commonly called Jacob's, or the Fatal Marble Stone, which is an oblong, of about 22 in. in length, 13 in. broad, and 11 in. deep; of a steel colour, mixed with some veins of red...

THE REGALIA.

These are—St. Edward's Staff—the Spurs—the Sceptre with the Cross—the Pointed Sword of Temporal Justice—the Sword of Mercy—the Sword of State—the Sceptre with the Dove—the Orb—St. Edward's Crown—the Patina, the Chalice, and the Bible.

THE CORONATION DAY.

All hail, Queen Victoria! all hail to this day,
So teeming with promise—we welcome it here!
As the bright stream of glory pursues its glad way,
And the blessing of thousands ascends in thin cheer!

SKETCH OF HER MAJESTY.

Her most gracious Majesty is the only daughter of the Duke of Kent, the fourth son of George III. and of the duchess of Kent, the sister of Leopold, king of the Belgians. She was born on the 24th of May, 1819, and had reached the age (eighteen) required by the law, before she could assume the reins of government...

Total Defeat of Bonaparte's Principal Generals.

Entrance of the Allies
INTO
PARIS.

FLIGHT *of the French* EMPRESS *And the* KING *of* ROME.

Proclamation in favour of the House of Bourbon.

ALL due thanks to the Almighty Disposer of Events—we have this week the supreme happiness of congratulating our Readers upon a series of Splendid Victories, the glorious heart-gladdening result of which is the Capture of the Capital of the French Empire, which was entered by the Allied Sovereigns, at the head of their Armies, on the 31st ult. conformably to a Capitulation for that purpose, duly

---

INSURRECTION
AT
PARIS.

FRIGHTFUL SLAUGHTER.

At length the fruit of the revolution of February is beginning to display itself. The " Men of the Barricades" who overthrew the monarchy have now turned against the Republican Government, and the blood-red days of the revolution of 1792 are re-enacting. The commencement of—or rather the immediate cause of the scenes of carnage we are about to relate, seems to have originated in the discontent of the *ouvriers*. The necessities as well as the convictions of the Executive Government had at length induced them to discharge from Paris on Thursday a draught of some thousands of the *ouvriers*, who were furnished with money for their journey and with billets for board and lodging at various points of their route to their homes

24 News from France (1). News of Napoleon's first defeat quickly spread to all parts of the country in 1814. Similar headlines appeared after his final defeat at Waterloo in 1815. (*Felix Farley's Bristol Journal*, 9 April 1814.)

25 News from France (2). The European revolutions of 1848 were widely reported in British newspapers. This headline owes much to the style adopted by *The Times*. (*Surrey Gazette* 27 June 1848.)

The People.

A Weekly Newspaper for All Classes.

ONE PENNY. [Registered for Transmission Abroad.]	LONDON, SUNDAY, OCT. 16, 1881.	110, STRAND.—No. 1.
SPECIAL	to act on the advice given them by Mr. Parnell. Mr. Metge, M.P., having seconded the resolution, it was passed. Other resolutions were adopted and the pro-ceeding concluded. The mob in the street behaved in	by train, leaving Cork at 5.30 p.m. The arrest was ac-complished as quietly as possible. The arrests are believed to be preliminary to the sup-pression of the Land League and the seizure of the	LATEST TELEGRAMS.

26 *right*. John Browne Bell's manifesto to Sunday readers, laid out in the first issue of the *News of the World*, 1 October 1843.

27 *above*. The mast-head of the first issue of *The People*. Like the *News of the World* it has concentrated on subjects far beyond the general sphere of politics. (*The People*, 16 October 1881.)

THE NEWS OF THE WORLD.
(FIRST EDITION.)

LONDON :
SUNDAY, OCTOBER 1, 1843.

TO THE PUBLIC.

A Few Words of Introduction.

We present to the Public, A NOVELTY IN NEWS-PAPER LITERATURE — *a Weekly Journal of the* Largest Size, *unexampled in point of Cheapness, and which, we trust, will be pronounced of the highest order of* merit. *Our object is to establish* A FIRST CLASS JOURNAL *at a Price which shall place it within the reach of* ALL CLASSES OF READERS. *Our arrangements have been made without regard to expense. And we encourage the hope that public opinion will pronounce* "THE NEWS OF THE WORLD" *the* BEST, *as well as the* LARGEST *and the* CHEAPEST *of all the Newspapers that are Published.*

We abstain from elaborate introductory observations. The contents of the Broad Sheet now in the hands of the Reader, will manifest our determination to avail ourselves of every means of making "THE NEWS OF THE WORLD" *most useful as a Political Guardian and Guide, and most in-teresting as a Newspaper to the general Reader. It is only by a very extensive Circulation that the Proprietors can be compensated for the outlay of a Large Capital in this Novel and Original Undertaking; but they are confident that Pub-lic Patronage will keep pace with desert, and that the nu-merous attractions—the intrinsic merits, as well as the ex-traordinary Cheapness of* "THE NEWS OF THE WORLD" *will be duly appreciated: and that, in point of Circulation this Paper will soon stand first among the most Popular, as no pains will be spared to establish its cha-racter as First among the Best of the Weekly Journals.*

WE MOST POSITIVELY AND DISTINCTLY STATE, THAT UPON NO ACCOUNT SHALL ANY ALTERATION EVER BE MADE IN THE PRICE OF "THE NEWS OF THE WORLD." WE INTEND, AND ARE RESOLVED, *that it* SHALL BE SOLD FOR THREEPENCE ONLY. *We dis-tinctly pledge ourselves to this. We enter into an inviolable compact with the Public, never to Charge for* "THE NEWS OF THE WORLD" *more than its present Price. One of the great features of the Publication is its Extraordi-nary Cheapness ; and this great feature shall never be in-terfered with, on any account whatsoever.*

We are induced to make the above declaration in emphatic terms, on account of the Price of Newspapers having been advanced, by degrees, after a certain Circulation has been

31

28 *left*. Middle and upper-class ladies had leisure enough to read *The Gentlewoman*. Christmas issues contained specially commissioned stories by well-known authors. The standards of design and colour printing were high. A free satin print was offered with this issue, of 1897 (compare 1, 2).

29 The *Illustrated London News* issued many special supplements. A few, like this one showing the Oxford and Cambridge boat-race teams, were printed in colour. (*Illustrated London News*, 29 March 1873.)

The newspaper and the 'media': the 20th-century phenomenon

In terms of the history of newspapers, the overlap of the nineteenth century and the present one might be said to end with the outbreak of the Great War. The press families and the barons of the last decade of the 19th century survived because their only competition was the spoken word. In common with other provincial owners the Scotts had created in the *Manchester Guardian* a force to be reckoned with. The Formans of Nottingham built up the *Nottingham Evening Post* into a newspaper with a county-wide circulation. In 1982 it still published ten daily area editions. Many towns were prosperous to such a degree that they could afford the luxury of two or more newspapers, sometimes owned by the same family interests, appearing as morning and evening editions or in direct political opposition to each other. They were still published in the traditional way. Reporters used the telegraph or the telephone to file their stories.

It was not until 1902 when Guglielmo Marconi invited *The Times* to participate in wireless experiments that the position began to change. Wireless, although in its infancy, was to demonstrate remarkable results. Despite strict Japanese censorship, *The Times* received wireless messages from its reporters on board a specially chartered steamer during the Russo–Japanese war of 1904–05. 'Dr' Hawley Harvey Crippen became the first murderer to be caught as a result of radio messages transmitted across the Atlantic in 1910. The novelty of the situation was exploited by the newspapers. The *Daily Mirror* even published a photograph of Crippen taken clandestinely in court in October 1910. The photograph is blurred but Crippen's figure seated in the dock can be clearly seen.

The true value of wireless was proven by the foundering of the RMS 'Titanic' on her maiden voyage in April 1912 (**30**). The newspapers had followed her construction closely, and they reported the sailing of this 'unsinkable' vessel. Radio signals picked up by Lloyds of London indicated the ship's difficulties. *Lloyd's List* published the messages from the White Star liner and other vessels steaming to her assistance. The *New York Times* gave over its front page to news of the shipwreck. The *Daily Mirror* and *Daily Sketch* published pictures of prominent personalities who died. These included W T Stead, former editor of the *Pall Mall Gazette*.

More technical innovations came about as a result of the Great War. Public radio broadcasting was born. In Britain the newspapers had nothing to fear from radio as its proliferation was strictly controlled by Act of Parliament. The British Broadcasting Company (later Corporation) started a national, regional and

30 *facing page.* Home rule for Ireland was forced off the front pages when the 'unsinkable' Titanic foundered in the Atlantic. The news was not believed publicly until radio signals were confirmed by the White Star Line. (*Daily Mirror*, 16 April 1912.)

The Daily Mirror

THE MORNING JOURNAL WITH THE SECOND LARGEST NET SALE.

No. 2,645.   Registered at the G.P.O. as a Newspaper.   TUESDAY, APRIL 16, 1912   One Halfpenny.

DISASTER TO THE TITANIC: WORLD'S LARGEST LINER SINKS AFTER COLLIDING WITH AN ICEBERG DURING HER MAIDEN VOYAGE.

Disaster has overtaken the great steamer Titanic, the world's largest and most luxuriously appointed vessel. The liner, which was the latest addition to the White Star fleet, left Southampton last Wednesday on her maiden voyage to New York, and was in the vicinity of the Newfoundland banks, to the south of Cape Race, when she struck an iceberg, an ever-present peril in those latitudes at this time of the year, and, after her passengers had been saved—sank. "Wireless" again demonstrated its immense value, assistance being summoned by this means. Above, the mighty vessel is seen leaving Southampton on Wednesday.—(D.M.P.)

Photo Talbot.

DINNER DRESS, BY BEER

eventually empire service under the watchful eye of its first Director General, John Reith. Advertising was not permitted, as the American experience of commercial radio stations in every major city had not won British governmental approval. The fledgling BBC won acclaim during the General Strike of 1926 by its provision of impartial news to a largely newspaper-less Britain.

The Times published a reduced edition, fighting off attempts by Winston Churchill to commandeer all of its newsprint to produce the *British Gazette*. (The latter propaganda sheet is housed with its adversary the *British Worker* in the Newspaper Library. Other short-lived attempts at printed communications have been preserved in a special collection of General Strike newspapers.)

During the Second World War the British Press was subjected to newsprint rationing which meant that every square inch of the page had to be usefully exploited. Most of the newspapers in support of the allied war effort finished the war in a healthy financial position. By the 1950s however, circulation figures had begun to decline – a factor which continued into the 1960s. Falling circulation meant falling advertising revenue, and much of this was due to the expanding worldwide coverage of news by BBC radio and television. Matters were not improved when another threat, in the form of British commercial television, started in 1955. Independent Television News provided an alternative news source, supplemented by Independent Radio News in the 1970s.

It has been a hard fight for national newspapers during the last 25 years. Many have changed from a broadsheet to a tabloid format. The *Daily Mail*, *News of the World* and *The Sun* have taken this option. Three London evening newspapers have been reduced to one. *The Star* and *Evening News* changed their format but this did not change their fortunes. *The Standard* eventually won the advertising battle. Besides the newspaper casualties, the other casualties have been the capital's reading public who no longer have a choice of evening newspapers.

The Sun's formula of sensationalised, simplified news together with a naked woman on page three and extensive sports coverage has transformed its position in the market. Its circulation increased from 1,065,972 to 4,150,191 in 16 years. It now has a rival in the *Daily Star* which first appeared in 1978 but so far has failed to wrest a major share of readers from *The Sun*. In the 1980s both of these newspapers, in common with the *Daily Mirror*, *Daily Express* and *News of the World* have offered daily bingo prizes as inducements to readers. The Fleet Street bingo phenomenon has grown to such an extent that standard prizes of £1,000,000 have evolved. Even *The Times* joined in with an up-market version based

31 The elegant lines of this 1912 couturier's creation appear quite modern. Coloured photoengravures of this type were pioneered on the continent before the Great War. (*Gallery of Fashion*, August 1912.)

DAILY EXPRESS

No. 14,094   Lighting-up: 9.39 pm to 4.33 am   TUESDAY AUGUST 7 1945   Weather: Cool, showers   One Penny

Smoke hides city 16 hours after greatest secret weapon strikes

THE BOMB THAT HAS CHANGED THE WORLD

Japs told 'Now quit'

THE Allies disclosed last night that they have used against Japan the most fearful device of war yet produced—an atomic bomb.

It was dropped at 20 minutes past midnight, London time, yesterday on the Japanese port and army base of Hiroshima, 190 miles west of Kobe.

The city was blotted out by a cloud of dust and smoke. Sixteen hours later reconnaissance pilots were still waiting for the cloud to lift to let them see what had happened.

The bomb was a last warning. Now leaflets will tell the Japanese what to expect unless their Government surrenders.

So great will be the devastation if they do not surrender that Allied land forces may be able to invade without opposition.

20,000 tons in golf ball

ONE atomic bomb has a destructive force equal to that of 20,000 tons of T.N.T., or five 1,000-plane raids. This terrific power is packed in a space of little more than golf ball size.

Experts estimate that the bomb can destroy anything on the surface in an area of at least two square miles—twice the size of the City of London.

When it was tested after being assembled in a farmhouse in the remote desert of New Mexico, a steel tower used for the experiment vaporised; two men standing nearly six miles away were blown down; blast effect was felt 300 miles away.

And, at Albuquerque, 120 miles away, a blind girl cried "What is that?" when the flash lighted the sky before the explosion could be heard.

In God's mercy we outran Germany

This statement was prepared by Mr. Churchill before he resigned, and was issued from Downing-street last night.

By WINSTON S. CHURCHILL

BY THE YEAR 1939 IT HAD BECOME WIDELY RECOGNISED AMONG SCIENTISTS OF MANY NATIONS THAT THE RELEASE OF ENERGY BY ATOMIC FISSION WAS A POSSIBILITY.

The problems which remained to be solved before this possibility could be turned into practical achievement were, however, manifold and immense; and few scientists would at that time have ventured to predict that an atomic bomb could be ready for use by 1945. Nevertheless, the potentialities of the project were so great that his Majesty's Government thought it right that research should be carried on in spite of the many competing claims on our scientific manpower.

At this stage the research was carried out mainly in our universities, principally Oxford, Cambridge, London (Imperial College), Liverpool and Birmingham. At the time of the formation of the Coalition Government [May 1940] responsibility for co-ordinating the work and pressing it forward lay in the Ministry of Aircraft Production, advised by a committee of leading scientists presided over by Sir George Thomson.

At the same time, under the general arrangements then in force for the pooling of scientific information, there was a full interchange of ideas between the scientists carrying out this work in the United Kingdom and those in the United States.

A REASONABLE CHANCE

Such progress was made that by the summer of 1941 Sir George Thomson's committee was able to report that, in their view, there was a reasonable chance that an atomic bomb could be produced before the end of the war. At the end of August 1941 Lord Cherwell, whose duty it was to keep me informed on all these and other technical developments, reported the substantial progress which was being made.

The general responsibility for the scientific research carried on under the various technical committees lay with the then Lord President of the Council, Sir John Anderson. In these circumstances (having in mind the effect of ordinary high-explosive which we had recently experienced), I referred the matter on August 30, 1941, to the Chiefs of Staff Committee in the following minute:—

GENERAL ISMAY FOR CHIEFS OF STAFF COMMITTEE—Although personally I am quite content with the existing explosives, I feel we must not stand in the path of improvement, and I therefore think that action should be taken in the sense proposed by Lord Cherwell, and that the Cabinet Minister responsible should be Sir John Anderson. I shall be glad to know what the Chiefs of the Staff Committee think.

The Chiefs of Staff recommended immediate action with the maximum priority.

I.C.I. MAN IN CHARGE

It was then decided to set up within the Department of Scientific and Industrial Research a special division to direct the work, and Imperial Chemical Industries, Ltd., agreed to release Mr. W. A. Akers to take charge of this directorate, which was called, for purposes of secrecy, the Directorate of "The Alloys."

After Sir John Anderson had ceased to be Lord President and became Chancellor of the Exchequer, I asked him to continue to supervise this work, for which he has special qualifications.

To advise him there was set up under his chairmanship a consultative council composed of the President of the Royal Society (Sir Henry Dale),

Experts worked at Bushy Park

By GUY EDEN

IN final vital link in the chain of experiments at led to the atomic mb is said to have been covered largely by accint and to have been ainly the work of British entists.

is considered advisable to ander the experiments to erica's vast open areas cause an explosion of the id created by the new exsive force would have doubtless caused great mage in Britain even if it were in some reof Scotland.

o the experiments were e at Teddington, Middlesex.

Underground

cientists realised that they dealing with a power so mense that it might have ed out the whole of that rk.

Even many close shaves ring the experiments which at throughout the blitz on n in England.

harles Darwin, director of the tonal research laboratory at lington, lives directly on the

none of Imperial College the —occupied by King William from—in the middle of London Park, and on the cellars the physical research laboraes there.

rrounded by experimental ments, the light does not ow that it might have drawn out the whole of that rk.

ype of security surrounds e Alloys depot.

he blind is either firing room floor bell.

scha has driven but to luck 'one—one from a laine on the atomic bomb.

'Under 400 lb.'

PRESENTATIVE of the istry of Aircraft Protion that it might was speaking

The men who knew

SIR JOHN ANDERSON
He supervised the work

SIR CHARLES DARWIN
He was called in

PLANE KIDNAPS SCIENTIST

Snatched from Nazis to help us

A DANE who was smuggled into Britain and two Germans who were hounded out of their country helped the Allies to perfect the atom bomb.

PROFESSOR NIELS BOHR is the Dane; one out of the men who isolated the first form of uranium known as U 235.

When the Nazis invaded Denmark they wanted him to carry on the atomic research that had won "him the Nobel prize. His answer—he stayed his laboratory and remained "underground."

The Gestapo hunted him. In October 1943 Resistance men whisked him past the Gestapo posts.

Twelve days he stayed in Sweden; guarded by squads of Swedish police from the ever-hunting Agents and the Gestapo.

A Mosquito bomber the "the German air" over Norway to pick up the professor and bring him to England.

Born and later in the U.S.A. Professor Bohr and his colleagues worked on the problems of the atom bomb, their whereabouts always secret. Only laboratories always guarded.

Professor Bohr is in Britain now—his whereabouts are no longer secret. He is in London.

TWO GERMANS

PROFESSOR RUDOLF PEIERLS and DR. FRANZ EUGEN SIMON are the German-born Jews who fled from Hitler's persecution and repaid Britain for her sanctuary.

Professor Peierls has been Professor of Applied Mathematics at Birmingham University since 1937. Other scientists who worked on the bomb were:—

SIR GEORGE PAGET THOMSON, 52, Professor of Physics at Imperial College of

PROFESSOR BOHR
The U 235 man—smuggled here from Denmark.

PROFESSOR FEATHER
Claims he was the first to split the uranium atom.

A widower with two daughters, lives Blackheath Gardens, Notting Hill Gate, W. then skiing and sailing.

DR. WALLACE ALAN AKERS, 57, a director of I.C.I., educated Lake House School, Bexhill; Aldenham School; and Christ Church, Oxford.

A bachelor, yachtsman. Lives in the Royal Thames Yacht Club.

TWINS

SIR JAMES CHADWICK, Professor of Physics at Liverpool University. He received science in 1932 by discovering an uncharged particle, the neutron, which completely changed conceptions of the constitution of matter. He is a Nobel Prize winner.

Married 1925, has wife and two daughters.

PROFESSOR J. D. COCKCROFT, Jacksonian Professor of Natural Philosophy, Cambridge. Thirteen years ago he broke up the atom by machinery, breaking the size of atomic energy for war, or for war; at 48, married and has a son and four daughters.

PROFESSOR NORMAN FEATHER of the Cavendish Laboratory, Cambridge.

BLAST FELT 300 MILES FROM BOMB TEST

Steel tower turned to vapour

From C. V. R. THOMPSON: New York, Monday

THERE is reason to believe that the vital part of the atomic bomb with its almost incredible power of devastation is not much bigger than a golf ball.

We have not seen it; all that is given officially—and this from the War Department—is that it is a revolutionary weapon destined to change war, or which may even be the instrumentally to end all wars."

But something is known about the first test, made in heavy rain at 5.30 a.m. on July 15 in a remote area of New Mexico.

We know that the blast was felt nearly 300 miles away. Imagine feeling in Piccadilly circus the effect of a bomb dropped in Penzance.

And here is this account, given by the U.S. War Department, of what happened in New Mexico:

"At the appointed time there came a blinding flash, lighting up the whole area brighter than the brightest daylight. A mountain range three miles from the observation point stood out in bold relief.

"There came a tremendous sustained roar, and a heavy pressure wave, which knocked down two men outside the control tower 10,000 yards—nearly six miles—from the scene of the explosion.

Vaporised

"Immediately afterwards a huge multi-coloured surging cloud boiled to an altitude of more than 40,000 feet. Clouds in its path, as it appeared, broke, shifting and showering rain, and then the surging cloud dispersed the narrow grey mass.

"The steel tower from which the bomb had been suspended had been entirely vaporised. Where the tower stood there was a huge sloping crater."

Specially equipped tanks, built to withstand great heat, brought into the area to examine the crater.

General Leslie R. Groves, one of the key men in the project, who was in the observation post when the bomb was exploded, was 10 miles from the tower, and said:—

"Two minutes before the explosion I heard Dr. Kistiakowski fling his face down with their feet pointing towards the explosion. As the roaring time had rolled away the men were permitted to gaze through their dark glasses. Even several feet of earth between us and the base of the explosion."

Ball of fire

"Dr. Conant, president of Harvard University, said that he had never imagined seconds could be so long, and that the observers, in accordance with orders, shielded their eyes.

"First came a burst of light of a brilliant beyond comparison. We all rolled over and looked through dark glasses at the ball of fire. About 40 seconds later came the great wave following the flash. The sounds, neither of which seemed startling after our complete astonishment at the extraordinary lighting intensity.

"Two explosions of minor effect other than lighting reached the sub-stratosphere—

► BACK PAGE, COL. ONE

THANKS, BRITAIN

Says Professor

From GUY AUSTIN

LOS ANGELES, Monday. Professor R. Robert Oppenheimer, director of the work on the atomic bomb, told me

4.30 a.m. LATEST

THE JAPANESE INVESTIGATE

Tokyo radio today said that the extent of the damage at Hiroshima "is now being examined."

JAP TOWN DESTROYED

GUAM, Monday.—The Japanese industrial town of Turuoka, on Kyushu, was completely destroyed yesterday in yesterday's raid by 180 Super-Forts.

Tonight that any success he may have had is greatly due "to the magnificent pre-war people in Cambridge University—a wonderful, wonderful place—did in teaching me.

"The professor was at Cambridge in 1925.

"We owe a profound debt of gratitude to your universities," he said. "The basic development of the science which made the atomic bomb possible was done in England and British scientists had always been generous

"From the laboratory where he had his atom smashing work, said he, the processor and, with great satisfaction, "I think we have done remarkably well.

LEFT HIS FARM

Professor Oppenheimer goes on to become foreman of a family that he has a ranch in New Mexico. But for the past three years he has worked on what we all have and had not since way back in the motion of the bomb.

As for the credit for a great nuclear physics—that is the brain which he was 40 per cent. British, but the 10th century of British-American

This ends war as we know it

Express Staff Reporter

THE Allied discovery ends war as we know it, because not only bombs, but torpedoes, gun shells and infantry weapons can be filled with atomic explosive.

Here is the principle: the atomic bomb strikes the uranium in it to disintegrate into millions of particles with enormous energy, moving at speeds like 186,000 miles a second. These outstanding particles coupled with the sudden liberation

THE WONDER OF THE WORLD

JAPAN

[map showing Hiroshima, Pacific Ocean]

HIROSHIMA (population 344,000) is one of the most important centres in Central Japan.

It was famed before today because in the bay outside the port is the sacred islet of Itaku-Shima — "Island of Light," which is regarded as one of the three wonders of Japan. The island has temple dating from 587.

of terrific heat came a catastrophic explosion.

The bomb probably contains less than an ounce of the pure metal uranium, which is converted to a constantly cooling of high-speed particles, but in small quantities.

What the scientists have done is

on stocks and shares called 'Portfolio'. The situation has its parallels in the circulation war waged during the 1930s by the national dailies. Then, book clubs were started or encyclopaedias and other part works were offered to readers. Many people accepted easy payment terms only to find that they were not always able to keep them up.

Elsewhere in Britain, provincial newspaper publishers have taken on the challenge of commercial radio and television on their own terms. Cable television franchises are supported and funded by prosperous provincial newspapers. The American experience of the 1930s has been repeated successfully in Britain. The free distribution newspaper has become a powerful force in local advertising and politics. The 'frees' are often supported by a sister newspaper paid for in the normal way. The advertising carried in the tabloid free newspaper helps to defray the costs of the other newspapers. Between them these free newspapers have taken advertising away from television and radio. Since the last war the cost of newsprint, which takes up 40 to 60 per cent of a newspaper's operating costs, has increased tremendously. Advertising rates have also risen, but circulation figures have also improved. Colour printing has been introduced by many provincial titles, such as *The Johnstone Advertiser*, as a regular feature. Smaller towns are often now left with one traditional newspaper. Rationalisation has caused the disappearance of old political rivalries, although independent newspapers have taken up a political stance in their locality to make their news coverage of local events more vivid. The feeling of 'community' is being advanced once more. Like their 19th-century counterparts, editors are always looking for a new appreciation of the latest town hall incompetence. The local correspondent has been supplemented by the individual who is encouraged to send in anything newsworthy for publication. Golden weddings still warrant a photographer and a couple of paragraphs.

Adoption of computer technology in many provincial editorial offices has meant a potential, if not actual, saving in manpower costs. The computer can be used to replace the hot metal process of the printing plant, and the journalist has the ability to type his own copy directly into a database. Advanced equipment can be used to set up pages on a computer screen, linked to an intelligent terminal for sub-editing. In theory then British journalists could be responsible, like their European and American colleagues, for the layout of the newspaper from the copy stage to the finished product. In reality not all of the traditional processes have been rendered obsolete by the computer. The national newspapers have resisted new technology, and many individual print chapels have come out

32 The dawn of the nuclear age. (*Daily Express*, 7 August 1945.)

Sporting Star

Saturday, February 23, 1985   Price 15p

FALCO FLOORS ALBION: ORMSBY 'SPECIAL'
KO'S HAMMERS: BLUES' RECORD DENTED

WOLVES' WAILS OF WOE!

With football out of the Deep Freeze today, there was little to put the icing on the cake for Wolves, Albion and Birmingham.

Wolves could only draw against Second Division bottom club Cardiff; Albion fell to a Mark Falco goal for Spurs, and Blues' away record was dented by Shrewsbury.

Delight, though, for Villa who won at West Ham with a 40-yard 'special' from Brendan Ormsby clinching the points, and Walsall who hit the goal trail in a penalty-clustered match against Orient.

WOLVES
BY DAVID Harrison

● WOLVES had to be content with a point when they so desperately needed three from their relegation crunch match against Cardiff at Ninian Park.

In the end they were happy to settle for a goalless draw for although they had chances of their own to sew up the game the best scoring opportunities fell the Welsh club's way.

Goalkeeper Tim Flowers was in his usual excellent form, twice keeping out point-blank efforts from Nigel Vaughan in the first half, while Wolves suffered an amazing escape in the 77th minute when Phil Dwyer's header hit the underside of the bar, and a rain of shots were cleared off the goal-line by Wolves defenders.

ALBION
BY DENIS SUNLEY

● ALBION, after making most of the running, fell behind to a 66th minute goal from Mark Falco in a thrilling duel with Spurs at the Hawthorns.

It was rough justice for

Albion who were much improved, appearing to have fully recovered from their disastrous spell in which they lost five of their last six matches before the Big Freeze.

They had to withstand heavy Hammers pressure in the opening half and, only three minutes after the break, Paul Goddard put West Ham ahead with an individual effort.

Villa, however, hauled themselves level in the 59th minute. Mark Walters did all the work on the left and appeared to be credited with the goal, although it might have taken a deflection from a West Ham defender on its way into the net.

And Brendon Ormsby snapped up a second goal 13 minutes from the end.

Albion's Garry Thompson on the burst at The Hawthorns this afternoon.

VILLA
BY PETER WHITE

● VILLA were under the cosh for nearly an hour against West Ham at Upton Park, but finally came alive after they had fallen behind.

away matches this season they were met by stiff resistance and a fine Paul Tester goal which gave Shrewsbury the lead.

Tester was easily the sharpest forward on the field with Birmingham making few scoring chances.

David Geddis threw away the two scoring opportunities they created in the first half

WALSALL
BY EDDIE GRIFFITHS

● WALSALL got right back into the promotion race after an untidy spell in the middle of the game. They were on the way to victory when Richard O'Kelly scored from a second minute penalty, but then they allowed Orient to level.

Craig Shakespeare recaptured Saddlers lead in the 16th minute and for the next hour Walsall lived dangerously.

Then O'Kelly scored a second penalty in the 77th minute and three minutes later Steve Elliott hit his first League goal since joining the club in November.

BLUES
BY TOM JOHNSON

● BIRMINGHAM'S hopes of setting post-war record of away League victories were stifled by a battling Shrewsbury at Gay Meadow. After winning two of their 13

GOAL CHART

Albion v Spurs
66—Falco .... 0—1

West Ham v Villa
44—Goddard .... 1—0
59—Walters .... 1—1
75—Ormsby .... 1—2

Liverpool v Stoke
14—Nicol .... 1—0
28—Dalglish .... 2—0

Shrewsbury v B'ham
40—Tester .... 1—0

Walsall v Orient
2—O'Kelly (pen) ... 1—0
14—Corbett .... 2—0
16—Shakespeare .... 2—1
77—O'Kelly (pen) .. 3—1
80—Elliott .... 4—1
86—Silkman (pen) .. 4—2

TODAY'S RESULTS AND TABLES

MILK CUP
Ipswich	1	Norwich	0

FIRST DIVISION
Arsenal	0	Man. Utd	
Coventry	1	Chelsea	
Leicester	1	Everton	
Liverpool	2	STOKE	
Newcastle	1	Luton	
Notts. For	2	S'th'mpton	
Q P R	1	Sunderland	
ALBION	0	Tottenham	
West Ham	1	VILLA	

SECOND DIVISION
Blackburn	1	Oxford	
Cardiff	0	WOLVES	0
Fulham	3	Carlisle	2
Grimsby	2	Notts Co	
Leeds	1	Charlton	0
Man. City	2	Brighton	0
Middlesbro	1	Hudd'field	2
Portsm'th	1	Oldham	1
Shef. Utd	3	Barnsley	1
SH'BURY	1	B'HAM	0

THIRD DIVISION
B'mouth	0	Reading	3
Brentford	0	Bristol C	0
Bristol R.	1	Plymouth	0
Burnley	2	Preston	0
Cambridge	1	Newport	2
Gillingham	1	York	0
Lincoln	2	Bolton	0
Millwall	4	Bradford	1
WALSALL	4	Orient	2
Wigan		Swansea	0

FOURTH DIVISION
Aldershot	2	Scunthorpe	
Blackpool	1	Southend	2
Bury	5	North'ton	1
Chester	5	Darlington	2
Crewe	1	Peterboro	2
Exeter	1	Halifax	
Hartlepool	2	Wrexham	0
Hereford	1	Torquay	
Port Vale	1	Stockport	2
Swindon	2	Rochdale	1

SCOTTISH FIRST
Airdrie	2	St John's'n	0
Ayr		Brechin	1
Clydebank	1	Hamilton	1
East Fife		Clyde	1
Mead'bnk	1	Forfar	
Motherwl	2	Kilmarnk	2
Partick	1	Falkirk	1

SCOTTISH PREMIER
Celtic	2	Aberdeen	0
Dundee U	4	Dumbarton	0
Hearts	2	Rangers	0
Morton		Dundee	
St. Mirren	1	Hibernian	4

FA TROPHY
Bangor	0	Stafford	

ALLIANCE PREMIER
Kidderminster	1	Barrow	
Weymouth	2	Telford	

SOUTHERN MIDLAND
Wellingboro	1	Stourbridge	
Merthyr	1	Dudley	
Sutton		Oldbury	
Bridgnorth		Leicester Ud	2
Hednesford		Redditch	

INTERMEDIATE
Birmingham	1	Villa	
Coventry		Notts Co	
Derby		Wolves	
Leicester		Stoke	
Mansfield		Shrewsbury	
Nottm Forest		Albion	
Port Vale		Walsall	1

FA VASE
Halesowen	1	Wythenshawe	

JOHN PLAYER RUGBY CUP
LYDNEY 4		SALE 29	
BATH 57		BLACKHEATH 3	
GLOUCESTER 29		SARACENS 3	
HARLEQUINS 16		LICHFIELD 4	
LIVERPOOL 9		LEICESTER 36	
MOSELEY 9		COVENTRY 29	
NOTTM 11		LONDON WELSH 12	
WATERLOO 21		WASPS 13	

WEST MIDLAND
WALSALL SENIOR CUP
Oldswinford	L	W'ton Utd	L
Harrison	L	Pelsall	L
Highgate	L	Brereton	L

Mich d'Avray delivers Milk

Mich d'Avray maintained his Milk Cup goal-a-round record for Ipswich today in their semi-final first leg clash with East Anglian rivals Norwich.

The South African-born striker headed in a George Burley free-kick after six minutes in front of a crowd of about 30,000 — the best at

Match off
● This afternoon's West Midlands premier division clash between Lye and Blakenall was postponed.

Portman Road for several seasons.

Ipswich, with England defender Terry Butcher in commanding form, were full value for their half-time lead.

TV FOOTBALL
BBC 1 (10.45 tonight): Blackburn v Oxford, Leicester v Everton, Ipswich v Norwich.

CENTRAL (2.30 tomorrow): Arsenal v Manchester United, Nottm Forest v Southampton.

At the top of the First Division, Everton and Tottenham were both finding it hard going away from home. Everton, the leaders, were drawing 0-0 at Leicester

33 Many provincial daily newspapers publish a special sporting edition on Saturday evenings during the football season. These are often printed on distinctive pink or pale-green paper. (*Sporting Star* (Wolverhampton). 23 February 1985.)

on strike in defence of their members' jobs. But time would not appear to be on their side. The new processes are already used by newspapers in the United States, Germany, Canada and elsewhere. Other countries are following slowly on the heels of the leaders. The savings are obvious; the typesetting procedures involved in the production of some British national newspapers are cumbersome, time-consuming and in general wasteful of manpower. Compared with their provincial competitors some national newspapers are anachronisms. Without modification and acceptance of new technology not all of the existing national dailies will survive until the end of this century.

Advertising

The struggle for survival has always been a fact of life in newspaper publishing. In the earliest days a printer could have ended up on the scaffold if he displeased the Star Chamber. Unlike today, when the sole objective of newspaper publishers is to print and sell a newspaper, the 18th- and early 19th-century newspaper owner was not fully employed by this task. He made his money by printing and selling books, broadsheets, ballads or simply stationery. His printing shop was a place where, to quote Thomas Aris of Birmingham, 'advertisements and authentic articles of intelligence' were 'thankfully received'. More often than not a country printer did not regard the newspaper as a going concern but merely as a sideline.

On average a handpress operated by two men could produce about 250 double-sided (i.e. 4-page) newspapers an hour and at most this could only be maintained for a few hours at a time. The printing operation was relatively simple, but difficulties arose when type had to be re-set in order to incorporate important news. This did not happen very often and it was customary for the small printer to hold over the news which arrived in the post on printing day, until the following issue. The topicality of the news was dependent upon the posts and what was contained in the letters and other newspapers. Should the post be delayed due to bad weather or highwaymen, the printer could be hard-pressed to fill his pages. Some publishers made the newspaper mast-heads very attractive. Woodblock or engravings showed prospects of the towns concerned. *Jackson's Oxford Journal* used an early engraving, and Ipswich appeared on the front page of the *Ipswich Journal* (18). As late as 1841 the *Sussex Advertiser* used the Brighton Pavilion in its mast-head (34), and vignettes of local places (35) to introduce local news.

To make ends meet the early editors resorted to advertisements. These were usually pre-paid, either in coin or in kind. The printer was also a stockist of the medicines and dyes, starches or boot-blacking which he advertised. He could ill-afford to be slow in advertising his own skills. As late as 1863 Robert Gibbs (who also worked as an insurance agent) placed a striking advertisement which spanned two columns of the *Bucks Advertiser* 31 October 1863 (36). The *Bath Chronicle* ran a series of woodblock advertisements of a Columbian hand press, which was obsolete for printing newspapers, but was used as an illustration (37). Perhaps the reader's mind could associate itself more readily with this type of press rather than the larger steam-driven multi-feeders or continuous reel presses (21). A similar advertisement had also appeared in the first edition of the *Newspaper Press Directory* in 1846. Then the

34 The Brighton Pavilion was the central image in the mast-head of the *Sussex Advertiser*. (8 March 1841).

35 Some printers whose newspapers covered a wide geographical area broke up closely-set columns with vignettes. News from the local districts was introduced by local scenes in the *Sussex Advertiser* (8 March 1841).

full working details of the press could be discerned. By the time the vignette had been used by Thomas Taylor in the *Bath Chronicle*, the image had become blurred. *Jackson's Oxford Journal* of 7 December 1754 (p.4) carried advertisements for wash-balls and printing ink 'which could be had of the printer'. The publisher of the *Kentish Weekly Post* was a purveyor of 'British Herb Snuff', and Original Herb Tobacco. Local druggists, shop-keepers and auctioneers took advantage of the circulation provided by the newspaper. Many papers were printed to coincide with market day, when advertisements for *Dr. Daffy's Elixir* or *Dr. Hooper's Female Pills* would perhaps have had maximum effect.

The London newspapers were fortunate to have a wider readership. The *Public Ledger* of 16 December 1795 advertised sales by candle at New Lloyd's Coffee House, of ships and their merchandise. Mr Christie advertised a sale by auction in the pages of the *Morning Post* of 4 January 1777, whilst on 11 February an advertisement for Dr Samuel Johnson's *Dictionary* appeared in the same newspaper.

By the 1820s the advertiser's technique had become more advanced; for example, the woodcuts depicting a flute player in *Jackson's Oxford Journal* (**41**) had been replaced by skilfully executed engraved blocks which were used repeatedly. (Advertisers were accustomed to paying for an allotted space on a specific page for a period of up to six months or more.) The *Liverpool Mercury* ran a series of advertisements connected with the Lancashire cotton trade, showing people at work. In the same newspaper a very striking image of an elephant holding a pistol with his trunk was used to advertise a circus in the issue of 21 February 1822 (**44**). Judging by the delights listed the show must have been worth watching! One Walsall stationer, W Henry Robinson of the Stamp Office, relied upon the skill of the block-setter in the *Walsall Observer* in the 1870s to ensure that his many advertisements popped up when the reader was least expecting them. How else would he have disposed of 100,000 envelopes, or gallon casks of ink at 10 shillings? Paper, books and the all-important name would be found on page one, three, and even under the times of church services.

36 As late as 1863 the publisher of the *Bucks Advertiser* was acting as an insurance agent. (*Bucks Advertiser*, 31 October 1863.)

Advertising was reaching many more people by the mid-19th century and the railway mania of the 1840s meant that more people could travel further much more quickly than had been possible previously. The potential of advertising a product 'nationally' was grasped by Charles Mitchell who published the first issue of the *Newspaper Press Directory* in 1846. The information contained in the forerunner to *Benn's Press Directory* is extensive. Every major town is entered and its newspapers listed. After 1856 the publication became more elaborate and the political bias of the newspapers, their circulation area and readership were all entered. The *Directory* is an extremely useful source for historians of the early newspaper.

W H Smith, the newsagent, used the railways to great effect from 1855 after the repeal of the Stamp Tax. Having negotiated agreements with the railway companies which gave his firm a monopoly on newspaper and book sales on railway stations, he introduced newspaper trains to facilitate speedy distribution (**45**). Readers in provincial towns and cities, or temporarily captive travellers, benefitted from this innovation. They now had a new slant on the news which had been confined previously to comment on their own town's papers.

In turn railway companies advertised in many newspapers, as stage-coach operators had done previously (**42, 43**). Details of cheap holiday excursions together with train timetables appear with great regularity, under illustrations of contemporary locomotives and carriages. Coastal newspapers featured ship news and advertisements for passages to Ireland or the continent (**46**). In 1846 and

37 An outmoded Columbia press advertised the latest types in Thomas Taylor's *Bath Chronicle*. Newspaper publishers all over the country acted as jobbing printers to keep their presses active. Spelling mistakes were usually corrected. (*Bath Chronicle*, 10 November 1864.)

The Public are respectfully informed that a
LARGE ASSORTMENT
OF THE
NEWEST TYPES
Has been Recently Added to the Stock at the
"CHRONICLE" OFFICE,
AND
PRINTING
Of EVERY DESCRIPTION
Can be Executed in the FIRS STYLE, at the LOWEST POSSIBLE RATES, and with DESPATCH.

At the Printing-Office in the High-Street, *and of the News-men, may be had*
The FAMOUS NEW INVENTED
Blacking Ball for SHOES,
Which for Neatneſs and Frugality, exceeds every other Preparation for that Purpoſe;

IT gives the SHOE a fine Gloſs, black as JET, and has the following excellent Properties: It will not in the leaſt dawb or ſoil the Fingers in putting on the Shoe, or the Stocking in wearing; it preſerves the Leather, keeps out the Wet, makes it always look like New, and cauſes it to wear a conſiderable Time longer, and is by far neater and cheaper than any common Blacking; one Ball uſed with Diſcretion being ſufficient to ſerve a ſingle Perſon a twelve Month.

Price One Shilling the large, and Six-pence the ſmall; with good Allowance to thoſe who buy them by the Groſe or Dozen to ſell again.

38 Another use for printing ink. (*Jackson's Oxford Journal*, 15 February 1755.)

1847 the *Belfast Newsletter* displayed illustrations of sailing ships above emigration notices, to entice a starving population to America. With the increasing use of steamers, these also appeared in the illustrations.

The development of transport and faster printing processes coincided with the rise in advertising agencies. The services which Mitchell was able to provide from London were taken up by the larger firms. Advertising returns and newspaper profits became dependent upon each other. A type of 'national advertisement' developed. Blocks could be cut in London and sent to newspapers anywhere in the country. Where no local stockist was needed and customers applied directly to the firm this posed no problem. One

The celebrated

ORMSKIRK MEDICINE,

Prepared by JAMES WARD, Surgeon and Chymist,

BEING the moft noble and fafe Antidote for the Bite or any Infection of

A MAD DOG,

39 The printer advertises his own wares – a patent medicine sold 'by the men who carry this Paper. Price 5s the Bottle'. (*Kentish Weekly Post*, 29 May 1769.)

For *MADEIRA*, *KINGSTON* and *OLD HARBOUR*,
The new Ship
PRINCESS CHARLOTTE,
Burthen 400 Tons—JAMES RAY, Master;
Will sail with the October convoy from Cork.
☞ For Freight or Passage apply to
ML. and J. F. ALEXANDER,
or the Captain on board.—Bristol, September 10, 1814.
☞ This Ship will take Wines in freight, from Madeira to Kingston and Old Harbour, and the voyage round, to be delivered in London.

Bor *BORDEAUX (without Convoy)*
The good Galias HEBE,
CHRISTIAN HARDER, Master;
Under a positive engagement to clear out on or before the 1st of October.
☞ For Freight or Passage apply to
Sept. 16.   ML. & J. F. ALEXANDER.

For *ROTTERDAM*,
The good Galias **LOUISA AMALIA**,
JACOB KRAEFFT, Master;
Having a great part of the cargo engaged, will sail with all dispatch.
☞ For Freight or Passage apply to
Sept. 24.   ML. & J. F. ALEXANDER.

40 Newspapers published in large ports could rely upon continuous shipping advertisements for revenue. The convoy system was applied to protect ships from the French. Ironically the advertisements provided Napoleon's navy with much information. (*Felix Farley's Bristol Journal*, 24 September 1814.)

GEORGE BROWN,

Wind Mufical Inftrument Maker, lately arrived from London, *at Mr.* Smith's, *the Harp and Crown in the* Old Butcher-Row, Oxford.

MAKES all forts of Wind Mufical Inftruments in the greateft Perfection, true and pleafant toned. To encourage Gentlemen to ufe his Inftruments he has likewife invented a new-fafhio ed Machine to fill the German Flute in every Note, from the loweft to the higheft; the like has not been performed by any Maker but himfelf in England. He likewife makes Hautboys, Baffoons, Clarnets, and Common Flutes in great Perfection ; efpecially a good Concert Common Flute, which is the Foundation of all Inftruments. Whoever deals with him may be fure of being well ufed.
N. B. *His Stay will be only one Week.*

41 Woodblock illustrations drew the reader's attention to an advertisement. This contemporary block may have been drawn originally from life. These types of illustration were later replaced by longer-lasting engraved blocks. (*Jackson's Oxford Journal*, 30 November 1754.)

VERY REDUCED FARES,
FROM THE
CROWN INN, REDCROSS-STREET, LIVERPOOL.

THE Public are most respectfully informed, that a New and Elegant Light Post Coach, called the CHAMPION (carrying only four insides) has commenced running from the above Inn, whence it leaves every morning at ten, and arrives the following afternoon, by four o'clock, at the Swan-with-two-Necks, Lad-lane, London.

The ROCKET, four insides, Coach, every afternoon, at three o'clock, through Birmingham, to the above Inn, in London. By this Coach, Passengers and Parcels are conveyed to Worcester, Gloucester, Bristol, Bath, Exeter, and Plymouth, on the lowest terms, and most expeditious manner.—Performed by   SAML. HENSHAW and Co.

N.B. Coaches to Manchester four times a day, the North of England and Scotland five times a day, from the above Inn.

42 Before the days of steam railways the post-coach was the only reliable means of rapid transport. The block cutter has succeeded in conveying the feeling of speed. (*Liverpool Mercury*, 10 May 1822.)

MIDLAND RAILWAY.

EXCURSIONS to the SEA-SIDE.—SCARBRO', HARROGATE, WHITBY, FILEY, BRIDLINGTON, REDCAR, SALTBURN, WITHERNSEA, The EASTERN COAST, SCOTLAND MORECAMBE BAY, BELFAST, DUBLIN, ENGLISH LAKES, NORTH WALES, ISLE OF MAN, MATLOCK BATH, BUXTON, MALVERN, &c.

43 The arrival of the railways did away with canal and coach traffic. Railway companies' advertisements replaced those of a previous age. The advertisements followed a pattern by including blocks showing a fully-laden train. Blocks were retained by the newspaper long after the trains themselves had been superseded. (*Bath Chronicle*, 1 September 1864.)

44 *right*. Before the invention of cinema and television our ancestors would relax at circuses or menageries. If the advertisement is to be believed, the elephant was a prodigy. (*Liverpool Mercury*, 21 February 1823.)

Menagerie.

By the request of several Parties of distinction, the Menagerie, Dale-street, corner of John-street, is reopened, and will continue to exhibit for a short time longer.

By permission of his Worship the Mayor.

NEVER HERE BEFORE.

NOW EXHIBITING, in DALE-STREET, near the Exchange, DRAKE and GILLMAN'S Royal Menagerie and Grand Depot of Animated Nature, never before exhibited in this kingdom, consisting of the most wonderful productions of nature, amongst which are the following:

That stupendous animal the PERFORMING ELEPHANT, from the Theatre-Royal, Covent Garden, London. His astonishing Feats of Performances are as follow:—He opens and shuts his own door; shows the company how he would liberate his master from prison; lies down at the word of command; takes up his Keeper upon his neck, carries him round the theatre, and shows the audience how the Elephant is fed when travelling, and lies down again for him to get off; takes a tea-kettle of boiling water off the fire assists the Keeper with it, and returns the kettle again to the flames; he will take a little pin from betwixt the finger and thumb of any baby, put it into his Master's pocket, take it from the mouth of his Master, and return the pin to the infant; takes a gentleman's hat off, and puts it on again; will take the smallest piece of money from any lady or gentleman, put it into the Keeper's pocket, and take it out of the Keeper's mouth, and return it to the same person who gave it him; he tells the time of the day; he shows what trade he would like to be; he shows the company how he would protect his Keeper from the ravages of wild beasts; he suffers the Keeper to put his head out of sight down his throat; and answers every question his Keeper puts to him; he also kneels down and thanks the company for coming to see him; with a variety of other performances too tedious to detail. *Fires off a Pistol!* The spectators will likewise have an opportunity of seeing the Elephant take his water, which is allowed by every person to be the greatest curiosity in nature. This animal weighs upwards of five tons weight, and stands nearly ten feet in height; his amazing bulk must strike every beholder with admiration. He is allowed by every visitor to be the largest Elephant in Europe. His consumption of food daily, is nearly *seven hundred weight*. This is not the Elephant that was here last, being three times its size. The one here presented to the public was procured by the Proprietor at an enormous expense. It is only nine years and a half old, remarkably tame, and one of those distinguished by the Indians of the east of Salona, which is the finest kind of Elephant in the world.

Two Living SERPENTS: the beautiful Great BOA CONSTRICTOR, which measures twenty-two feet in length, and twenty-four inches in circumference. He is so remarkably tame that the most timid person may handle him without danger; he exceeds all the Serpent species in beauty as well as strength. Also, the wonderful Aquatic SEA SERPENT ALIVE! the only one travelling in this kingdom, which was discovered when they were out in search of the great one, and is supposed, by moderate calculation, to measure *more than 300 feet in length*, and which they frequently saw, but could not succeed in taking. From the circumstance of finding the one now brought to England near Cape Ann Harbour, it is asserted by the Linnæan Society that it is of the same breed as the large one.

SIX NOBLE LIONS, among which is a full-grown majestic MALE LION, which instantly impresses every beholder with that magnificent idea so generally conceived of the king of the brute creation. His form is strikingly bold and majestic, having a large shaggy Mane, which he can erect at pleasure, and whose roaring, like thunder, exhibits a picture of grandeur which no words can describe. Three Noble BRITISH LIONS, which were Cubbed on the 1st of June, 1822.

Also, a beautiful real ZEBRA, in which it seems as if the most exquisite works of art had been combined with nature

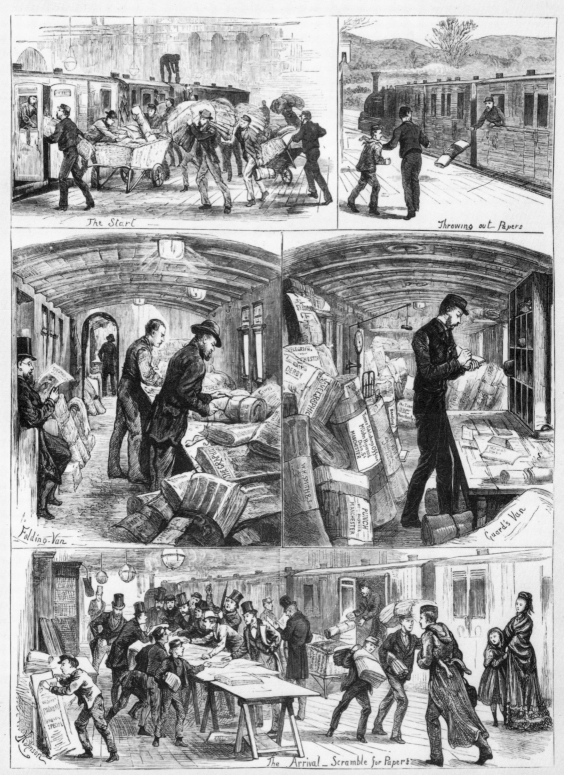

The Start

Throwing out Papers

Folding-Van

Guard's Van

The Arrival — Scramble for Papers

NOTES IN AN EARLY NEWSPAPER TRAIN

such company was J W Benson of Ludgate Hill, London. Its advertisements in the 1860s for watches and clocks, and Benson's Argentine Silver were to be found in newspapers like the *Bucks Advertiser* and the *Cumberland & Westmorland Advertiser*, published at opposite ends of England. Part of this success can be attributed to the London newspapers' provision of pages whose contents of news and advertisements could be integrated into the provincial newspaper. Thus the 'national' newspaper was taking shape, within a regional context.

It was not impossible to alter part of an advertisement in order to retain the illustration but provide the name and address of the local stockist. Readers would discover *Mazawattee Tea* or *Beecham's Pills* advertisements in the classified columns as well as on the front page.

Always 'worth a guinea a box', Beecham's Pills were promoted heavily through newspapers and the better-class ladies' periodicals such as *The Queen* or *The Gentlewoman*. At one stage in the 1890s Thomas Beecham employed a clever advertising agency which used adaptations of music-hall songs and a full-page illustration. The one entitled 'Oh, Mister Porter' accurately shows railway carriages, soldiers and sailors, the distressed lady passenger and of course, the railway porter. Advertisements for the all-important pills are posted up all over the station. Another shows an attractive woman using the early telephone (**47**).

Coloured photogravures were used by Pear's Soap. The most famous is the 'Bubbles' advertisement which exploits Sir John Millais' portrait. Other black and white advertisements depicted a grubby, reluctant boy subjected to a good scrubbing by an elderly servant under the heading 'You dirty boy' (**49**).

45 *left*. The nation's desire for news was satisfied daily by W H Smith who chartered the first newspaper trains to transport London newspapers and other major provincial titles all over the British Isles. (*The Graphic*, 15 May 1875.)

46 As steam ships became more common, the vignettes in newspapers altered to take this into account. By the mid-nineteenth century steam and sailing vessels could be found side by side. (*Liverpool Mercury*, 17 May 1822.)

SUPERIOR TRAVELLING, TO DUBLIN & BRISTOL.
THE new and elegant Liverpool-built Steam Packet ST. PATRICK, J. P. PHILLIPS, R. N. Commander, Sails every Tuesday morning at Seven o'clock, for Dublin, and arrives there the same evening; landing her passengers, without reference to the time of high water. On Wednesday, at Twelve o'clock at noon, she proceeds from Dublin to Bristol, calling at Tenby, on her route, and will arrive at Bristol on Thursday afternoon.
Passages engaged on application to
JOHN WATSON, Jun. 27, Water-street.
The ST. GEORGE Steam Packet, of the same size, power, and equipment, will sail for the Isle of Man, Portpatrick, and Greenock, on Monday morning, the 3d of June, at Ten o'clock, and continue to sail weekly during the season.
(One concern.)

Are you there?

Don't Forget TO BUY Beecham's Pills.

FOR ENSURING A CLEAR COMPLEXION, BEECHAM'S PILLS STAND UNRIVALLED.

BEECHAM'S PILLS are, without doubt, the most marvellous Medicine in the world for BILIOUS and NERVOUS DISORDERS, SICK HEADACHE, CONSTIPATION, WEAK STOMACH, IMPAIRED DIGESTION, DISORDERED LIVER, and FEMALE AILMENTS.

The Sale now exceeds 6,000,000 BOXES PER ANNUM.

Published by Mr. ALEX. J. WARDEN, for "THE GENTLEWOMAN," Ltd., at the Offices, Effingham House, Arundel Street, Strand, and Printed by ODHAMS, LIMITED, 19—34, Floral Street, Covent Garden, London, W.C.

The
World's Record
BEATEN BY THE AID OF
St. Jacobs Oil.

MESSRS. S. B. McGREGOR AND G. A. NELSON.
Photo by EDGAR SCAMELL, 120, Crouch Hill, London, N.

Messrs. S. B. McGregor and G. A. Nelson
(Holders of the One Hour World's Record Tandem for all types of Cycles) write:—

" Now that we have used your famous St. Jacobs Oil every day for the past ten months, we are pleased to testify to its ... 1,550 yards, but 'World's Record' for all types of cycles, doing 31 miles 610 yards, the . . .

47 Advertisers have always combined femininity and new technology to promote products. This was one of a series produced for Beechams. (*The Gentlewoman*, Christmas Number 1899.)

48 *right*. During the 1880s and 1890s the working classes discovered a new independence provided by the bicycle (and tandem!). No longer were they totally dependent upon time-tabled trains. (*Golfing and Cycling Illustrated*, 28 October 1897.)

The two world wars caused shortages and rationing, but advertisements still reached the public. Raleigh cycles and Humber motor vehicles, for example, were portrayed in terms of the contribution they were making to the war effort; the civilian was made aware of the quality of the goods and the job that was being done with the product. Despite rationed newsprint the newspaper publisher was still able to bring in advertising revenue.

Over the last 30 years the newspaper has become a major local advertising medium. Television and commercial radio stations used to have the largest share of the lucrative national market, but now local newspapers have developed the full potential of their circulation.

Pears

YOU DIRTY BOY! (Another Version.)

PEARS' SOAP is absolutely pure, free from excess of alkali (Soda), and from artificial colouring matter. It is specially recommended for Infants and Children, because being pure it does not irritate their delicate sensitive skin, nor make their little eyes smart. It lasts so long that **it is certainly the CHEAPEST as well as the BEST Toilet Soap.** It makes Children feel comfortable, and hence happy after their bath, and by its use the natural softness and brightness of their complexions are improved and preserved.

Advertising and newspapers came of age together in the 19th century and their relationship is still very closely intermingled. Without each other the newspaper publisher and the local advertising agencies would very soon go out of business. As long as newspapers continue to be read for their news, advertisers will want to use them to reach their market.

THE "ROYAL MAIL,"

For Construction, Finish, and Excellence, of Manufacture The "ROYAL MAIL" is unsurpassed.

Price Lists can be obtained from the Manufacturers—

THE ROYAL SEWING MACHINE CO., (LIMITED), SMALL HEATH, BIRMINGHAM, .

Makers of Sewing Machines, Bicycles, and Tricycles.

THE TRIAL OF WM. CORDER

FOR

THE MURDER OF MARIA MARTEN.

LIKENESS OF WILLIAM CORDER.

THE RED BARN,
THE SCENE OF THE MURDER, AND WHERE THE BODY OF MARIA MARTEN WAS FOUND CONCEALED.

NORFOLK CIRCUIT:—SUFFOLK ASSIZES.

BURY ST. EDMUND'S, THURSDAY, AUGUST 7.

The anxiety to witness the trial of William Corder, was manifested by the assembling of hundreds of well-dressed persons, of both sexes, round the front and back entrances to the Shire Hall, at the early hour of five o'clock in the morning; and notwithstanding the rain continued to fall incessantly, they remained (except those who were carried away in a state of exhaustion from the pressure of the dense crowd) till nine o'clock, when the Lord Chief Baron (Alexander) arrived near the Hall. The external regulations were so bad, that nearly a quarter of an hour elapsed before the few Javelin-men who were in front

prisoner, but it was not until within twelve months before the 18th of May, 1827, that they became intimate; the result of which was the birth of an illegitimate child. The young woman was not confined at her father's house, but was removed to a distance; and about six weeks before the period in question, she returned home with her infant child. The child, which I believe had been always weakly, died in a fortnight after her return. It is right that I should here tell you that Corder had been heard to tell Maria Marten that the parish-officers were thinking of having her taken up because of another bastard child of which she had been delivered; and after her delivery of a child to him, he was heard to make to her the same declaration. Some difference was also known to exist between them with respect to a five-pound note. But of these facts they would hear more from the witnesses. On one occasion, before the 18th of May, last year, Maria Marten was heard to say to the prisoner—" Well, if I go to gaol, you shall go too." Corder, upon that occasion, told her he should make her his wife. On the Sunday before the 18th of May (which was a Friday), Corder called at her father's house, and told her they would go to Ipswich the next day and get married; but they did not go on that day. On Friday, the 18th of May, the prisoner called again at the house of the deceased, who was at the time up stairs with her mother; he called to her and said, "I am now going—are you ready?" She said "I cannot go out in the day time, people will see me." He told her that he had been disappointed several times, and that she must prepare and go then. It was arranged that she should put some clothes into a bag, which he would take to the Red Barn, to which she was to repair in male attire, to escape observation; and she could there change her dress, and proceed with him to Ipswich, where he would marry her. She put her dress into the bag, and also a small basket, into which she put a black velvet bag or reticule, lined with silk. Corder left the house, and was absent about a quarter of an hour, and on his return Maria Marten had habited herself in a coat, waistcoat and trowsers. She had also on a part of her own dress, consisting of a flannel petticoat and stays, with an asben busk; she wore ear-rings and a comb, and had round her neck a green handkerchief. They left the house at the same time, but by different doors, both going in the direction of the Red Barn. From that period the friends of Maria Marten never saw her again alive; nor did they hear anything of her, save such accounts as had been furnished them by the prisoner, and which accounts will be given to you in evidence. Before she left her home, he told her he had received a letter from a person named Balham, who would take her into custody on the ground of her having an illegitimate child; but Balham will tell you that he never gave the prisoner any such letter. On the day of her leaving her father's cottage for the Red Barn, a younger brother of her's, who was getting some grass in an adjoining field, saw the prisoner going towards the Red Barn with a pick-axe on his shoulder. This, Gentlemen, you will find to be a material circumstance in the case. The next time the mother of the deceased saw the prisoner was on the following Saturday, but nothing particular occurred on that occasion. On the Sunday she again saw him; he told her that he had not yet married her daughter; he said he had got the license, but that it was necessary to send it to London, and that in the mean time he had placed Maria with some friends of his, who resided at Yarmouth. She again saw the prisoner in the following week, and she told him of her son's having seen him go towards the Red Barn on the 18th of May with a pick-axe on his shoulder. But he said " it could not be me, it must have been a man named Acres, who was stubbing up some trees in a field near there." Now Acres will be called before you, and he will tell you that he was never so employed in that neighbourhood. Between the 18th of May, and up to the harvest time, the family of the deceased frequently saw the prisoner, and he assured them that she was still living with his friends, who, he said, were named Rowling. He represented her as being in good health; and when her friends complained of her silence, he accounted for it in various ways: at one time he said, when he was with her she was so much occupied with him that she had not time to write; at another, that she had a sore hand, and was unable to write; in a word, he continued to amuse her friends by various statements up to the harvest time. On one occasion he got into conversation with a female named Stowe, who lived near the Red Barn; Stowe asked him if Maria Marten was likely to have any more children, and he said she was not. Stowe asked why not? & observed that Maria was a young woman, and likely to have many more; but he said " No," she would not have any more; she had had her number. Stowe asked if Maria was any where near, and he replied; " she is where I can see her any day, and when I am not with her, I am sure nobody else is." There is another circumstance which, though trifling in itself, I feel it

Crime reporting

Advertisements have been the true revenue earners, but without news to interest readers, the newspaper would have no *raison d'être*. A study of the newspapers of three centuries will soon reveal to the reader that events repeat themselves. Only names and places change. Sensationalism is a device used by the newspaper editors with which the 20th-century reader has grown up. It is not new. The 'exclusive' tags given to stories by *The News of the World* or *The Sun* were preceded in the 1880s by W T Stead's *Pall Mall Gazette*. He showed the corruption and abuses in his society and sensationalised them by exploiting the criminal elements in the stories.

Crime was with us long before the newsletter or newspaper appeared. It is a type of story which has always held a fascination for readers, and editors have never been slow to exploit the fact.

Ordinary criminals were occasionally worthy of an illustration in *The Times* or *The Observer*. Other newspapers such as the *Weekly Chronicle* or *Bell's Life in London* were forerunners of the *Penny Illustrated Paper*, the *Illustrated Police News* (**52, 53**) and the *Illustrated Police Budget*. The word 'police' in the title was an indication of the contents. This type of publication appeared at weekends, published on a Saturday for Sunday. They were publicly criticised by religious opponents for defaming the sabbath with murders, robberies and sporting stories. But Sunday would have been the only day the working-classes had free, and they were the people who bought the 'sensational' press. Crime caught the country's imagination. The so-called 'Murder in the Red Barn' was given full treatment in *The Observer* of 1828. A full-length portrait of Maria Marten's murderer, William Corder, was published on 17 August 1828 together with other scenes of the crime (**51**). Over two weeks the reporter gave a verbatim account of the trial, and the reading public was presented with the lovers' meeting, the murder and the subsequent execution of Corder. Every newspaper in the area tried to cover the execution. Corder's penitence and demeanour at his death were recorded in detail.

Executions were popular spectacles for the general public. The execution of William Burke was described in *The Atlas* of 1 February 1829. Burke and Hare were murderers who sold their victims' bodies to a Dr Knox for dissection. After Hare had turned King's evidence, Burke was convicted and sentenced to be hanged.

The Times was not slow in reporting a murder or other type of crime; indeed, Barnes (editor from 1817–1841), thought that it added balance to the newspaper. *The Times* index for 1794 lists reports of 83 instances of actual or attempted highway robbery.

51 William Corder as *The Observer*'s artist saw him. The editor received complaints from readers who considered the dashing figure of the murderer distasteful. (*The Observer*, 11 August 1828.)

52, 53 *overleaf.* 'The Tunbridge Wells Crimes'; 'The Walthamstow Mystery Barber'; and of course 'Jack the Ripper'. Popular Crime Stories in 1888 editions of the *Illustrated Police News*.

POLICE THE ILLUSTRATED NEWS

LAW COURTS and WEEKLY RECORD

No. 1,289.   SATURDAY, OCTOBER 27, 1888.   Price One Penny.

SKETCHES OF THE TUNBRIDGE WELLS CRIMES.

SETTING FIRE TO A HAISTACK. — DESTROYING THE JUBILEE TREE. — ATTEMPTED MURDER OF A COMPANION. — PORTRAITS OF THE TWO PRISONERS DOBELL GOWER — SINGING IN PRISON. — WHY DON'T YOU CHARGE FOR ADMISSION? QUITE AT HOME IN THE DOCK. — DOBELL SHOOTING B. C. LAWRENCE THE TIMEKEEPER — SETTING FIRE TO A HOUSE. — COMMITTING BURCLARY.

LATEST INCIDENTS IN CONNECTION WITH THE DOINGS OF JACK THE RIPPER THE EASTEND FIEND.

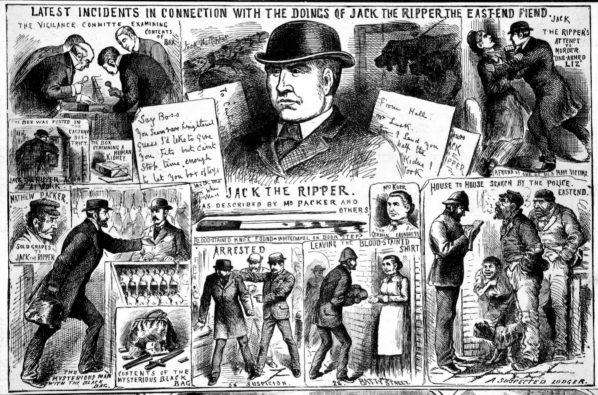

THE VIGILANCE COMMITTE EXAMINING CONTENTS OF BOX — THE BOX WAS POSTED IN THE EASTERN DISTRICT. — THE BOX CONTAINING A HUMAN KIDNEY. — JACK THE RIPPER AGAIN AT WORK. — JACK THE RIPPER'S ATTEMPT TO MURDER "ONE-ARMED LIZ" — A FRIEND OF ONE OF HIS MANY VICTIMS. — MATHEW PACKER. SOLD GRAPES TO JACK THE RIPPER. — JACK THE RIPPER. AS DESCRIBED BY MR PACKER AND OTHERS. — BLOOD-STAINED KNIFE FOUND IN WHITECHAPEL ON DOOR STEP. — ARRESTED ON SUSPICION. — LEAVING THE BLOOD-STAINED SHIRT. 28, BATTY STREET. — MRS KUER THE GERMAN LAUNDRESS. — HOUSE TO HOUSE SEARCH BY THE POLICE. EASTEND. — A SUSPECTED LODGER. — THE MYSTERIOUS MAN WITH THE BLACK BAG. — CONTENTS OF THE MYSTERIOUS BLACK BAG. — Say Boss You seem rare frightened guess I'd like to give you fits but can't stop time enough to let you box of toys — From Hell Mr Lusk Sor I send you half the Kidne I took

FATALITY ON THE RAILWAY! — ANOTHER DISCOVERY IN WHITEHALL BY A DOG — ATTEMPTED MURDER AND SUICIDE.

THE ILLUSTRATED POLICE NEWS

LAW COURTS AND WEEKLY RECORD

No. 1,277.

SATURDAY, AUGUST 4, 1888.

Price One Penny.

THE WALTHAMSTOW MYSTERY BARBER IN THE DOCK STRATFORD PETTY SESSIONS

MRS FRENCH'S LAST VISIT TO THE CHEMIST'S SHOP

THE BOY FETCHES BRANDY

BACK DOOR

THE ERRAND BOY GETTING OVER THE BACK WALL

ARREST OF BARBER ARRIVAL AT WALTHAMSTOW STATION

BARBER BREAKS DOWN IN THE DOCK

SUSPECTED AT THE COFFEE HOUSE

EXCITING CHASE AFTER A SUPPOSED BURGLAR.

PROFESSOR BALDWIN LEAPING FROM A BALLOON

PROF. BALDWIN.

CHARGE OF TORTURING A CAT.

ATTEMPTED MURDER AND SUICIDE.

In recent times, certain crimes have excited the emotions of those people who wait outside courts for murderers to emerge. Feelings have run so high that criminals have needed protection by the police. One such criminal was Peter Sutcliffe, convicted of the 'Yorkshire Ripper' murders. His Victorian predecessor was never caught. The Whitechapel Murderer or 'Jack the Ripper' has been immortalised in print for the hideousness of his crimes. Contemporary attempts to identify the killer were published in the *Penny Illustrated Paper* and *The Illustrated Police News*. Gory pictures of women lying in pools of blood with their throats cut and apprehended suspects were featured on the front pages (**52, 53**). The *Daily Telegraph* gave the Whitechapel Murders excellent coverage in a non-sensational manner.

Other crimes take on an aura of romance, perpetuated by the media. The so-called Great Train Robbery of August 1963 was such an event. *The News of the World* gave it front-page prominence with a headline which proclaimed 'How the great rail robbery was planned' on 11 August 1963. The *Daily Herald* showed the 'Robbers' hide-out' three days later. Five years after the robbery *The News of the World* ran another exclusive, 'Mrs Charlie Wilson tells the lot', on 25 February and 31 March 1968. Ronald Biggs, who escaped to Brazil, has evaded capture for so long that the national press has turned him into a Dick Turpin type 'folk-hero'.

54 *facing page.* The 'sensational' trial of Isaac Blight prompted *The Times* to print its first front-page illustration. (*The Times*, 9 April 1806.)

Mr. BLIGHT's HOUSE.

Ground Plan of Mr. BLIGHT's House.

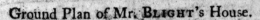

Narrow Passage behind the House.

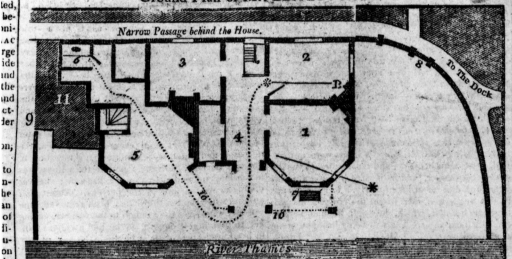

River Thames

1. Front Parlour, into which the first Shot was fired.	[The Positions of *Patch* when he fired the first and second
2. Back Parlour, in which Mr. Blight was shot.	Shots are marked by stars.]
3. Kitchen, from the Window of which the Maid Servant	[The situation of Mr. Blight when shot is marked B.]
jumped into the narrow Passage.	7. Cellar-door.
4. Entrance.	8. Wicket-gate.
5. Counting-house.	9. Stone-Mason's-yard.
6. Privy.	10. Railing in front of the House.
[The Way from the Privy to the back Parlour is described	11. Outhouses.
by a dotted line.]	

some days in the house, which being granted, he   commission of the crime. The enquiry was natural:

THE MAFEKING MAIL
SPECIAL SIEGE SLIP.

ISSUED DAILY, SHELLS PERMITTING. TERMS : ONE SHILLING PER WEEK, PAYABLE IN ADVANCE.

No. 70 Saturday, February 10th, 1900. 121st Day of Siege.

The Mafeking Mail.

SATURDAY, 10TH FEBRUARY, 1900.

LADYSMITH RELIEVED ?

Although there is no definite information to hand about Ladysmith, one may adopt, with feelings of confidence, the assumption that its relief has already been effected. We think on or about Wednesday, the 24th January. Space will not permit of giving the various pegs upon which to hang that belief, but Buller's advance on the 17th, the report of fighting at Spions Kop, on the 22nd and 23rd, the statement made in the paper of the 26th as to fighting having taken place 30 or 40 miles North of Ladysmith, the particular viciousness of the Boers here on the 27th to 31st. The London wire of the 2nd February telling of the upward bound on the Stock Market, all suggest that there is good news for us somewhere on the road.

With deep regret we record the death of Mr. James Dall, Town Councillor. All Mafeking will join in heartfelt condolence with his family in this their hour of sorrow and bereavement, and none will withhold tribute to the sterling integrity, the intense devotion as husband and father, and the worth of our late townsman.

POSTPONEMENT.

We are desired by Mr. Feltham, who is acting as Secretary to the Bachelor Officers Dance Committee, to state that as a tribute of respect to the family and friends of the late Mr. Dall, the dance announced for this evening will be postponed till to-morrow.

AUCTION SALE.

The undersigned, duly instructed, will sell by Public Auction, on

Sunday Next,
At 10-30 a.m.,

A quantity of Ladies and Mens Boots and Shoes,
Mens Underwear,
Trousers, Jackets, Shirts,

And many other articles too numerous to mention.

Also a lot of New and Second hand Novels.

In addition to the above a lot of
GOOD SECOND HAND CLOTHING

With the sanction of the Col. Commanding

CYCLE SPORTS

will be held at the

RECREATION GROUND,

— ON —

Sunday, February 11th,

Commencing at 2-30 p.m.

Lady Sarah Wilson has kindly consented to distribute the prizes, which comprise : *Watches ; a Clock ; a most handsome hand-painted "Watteau" Fan ; Silver Glove Buttoner ; Candlestick Mirror ; Silver mounted Pipes ; Amber Cigarette Holders ; Cigarette Cases, &c.*

Referee : H. H. Major Goold-Adams.
Judges : Major Godley ; Capt. Cowan.
   Inspector Marsh.
Handicappers : Lieut. Colonel Walford ;
   Inspector Browne.
Starter : C. G. H. Bell, Esq., C.C. & R.M.
Clerk of Course } To be appointed on
Lap Scorer }   the Ground.

The Totalisator

Will be upon the Grounds.
Under charge of Sergt. Major Merry.

PROGRAMME :

		Start.
1. One Mile Siege Championship		2-40
2. Team Race of One Mile ...		3-0
Four members of : The Prot. Regiment, the B.S.A. Police, the Cape Police, the Bechuanaland Rifles, and the Town Guard.		
3. Half Mile Bicycle Race in Fancy Costume.		3-20
One prize for Winner, and one prize for best Fancy Dress.		
4. Half Mile Ladies Race	...	3-40
5. Three Lap Race	... ...	4-0
Walk a lap.		
Ride a lap.		
Run a lap.		
6. One Mile Bicycle Handicap		4-40

POST ENTRIES.

Bicycles will be provided for those who have not their own. Lots being drawn for them.

The distribution of Prizes will take place directly after the last race.

By the kind permission of Capt. Cowan the Band of the Bechuanaland Rifles will play during the intervals.

Book Early for the

GRAND SIEGE CONCERT

UNDER THE PATRONAGE OF

Colonel R. S. S. Baden-Powell and Officers of the Garrison,

AT THE

MASONIC HALL,
February 11th, 1900,

TO CELEBRATE

THE 18TH SUNDAY OF THE SIEGE.

Commencing at 5-30 p.m.

Proceeds to be given to the Sports and Prizes Funds.

PROGRAMME :

PART I.

1. Cape Police, D. H., Khaki Band
2. Song ... "Anchored," Mr. Campbell
3. Pianoforte Recital,
   Signor Paderewski.
4. Song, "At the Ferry," Miss Friend
5. Mandoline Solo, "Mary" Waltz,
   Pte. J. P. Murray
6. Song, "Beauty's Eyes," Mr. Bulleid
7. Siege Song ... Pte. E. W. Coxwell
"If it wasn't for the Maxim in between,"

Interval of 5 Minutes.

PART II.

1. Piccolo Solo ... Mr. Westland
2. Leger de main ... Mr. F. J. Jacobs
3. Song, "Sunshine above,"
   Capt. Ryan, D.A.A.G.B.
4. Recitation, "Bill Tinka,"
   Lieut. C. X. McKenna.
5. Siege Sketch ... Gentleman Joe
6. Song, "The Outpost," Mr. Campbell
7. Comic Song ... Pte. E. W. Coxwell

God Save the Queen.

Owing to time no encores will be allowed.

HURRAH !!

Here is something Good.

F. FIRTH

Has still some hundreds of

Pianoforte Pieces and Songs

AT 4 COPIES FOR 1s.

ACCORDEONS

Gaining an empire

As British trade with the rest of the world increased, opportunities arose for merchants to set up branch offices in the newly exploited colonies. London and Bristol newspapers gradually found their way with the post to the expanding settlements in North America, India and later South Africa and Australia. By the mid-18th century America and Bengal had English-language newspapers. The Spanish and Portuguese settlers also produced their own newspapers in their colonies in Latin America. Newspapers thus played their part in the extension of European culture beyond its frontiers. Eventually they also penetrated China and Japan, where printing and paper had originally been invented.

British dominance in India was achieved only after prolonged conflict with the French and with native rulers. The East India Company administered Bengal and used *Hickey's Bengal Gazette* to promulgate decrees and notices, which Hickey published along with items from British newspapers. Like his English contemporaries Hickey had to make a living as a jobbing printer, preparing and printing forms for the East India Company's local administrators. Advertisements published in English, Hindi and Bengali were published in *Hickey's Bengal Gazette* and the *Calcutta Gazette* (56). Those few issues held in the Newspaper Library exhibit beautiful and serviceable Arabic and Bengali typefaces.

The British Library India Office Library and Records (IOLR) was entitled to receive copyright copies of items published in India, Ceylon and Burma between 1867 and 1948. Newspapers were included in this and the expatriate printers who founded the English-language titles sent them back to the IOLR and the British Museum. Many newspapers today survive uniquely in these collections.

Early American newspapers have also been preserved by the Newspaper Library. The *Massachussets Centinel* and *New York Journal*, like *Hickey's Bengal Gazette*, modelled their typographical layout on contemporary London newspapers. Parliamentary reports are found along with the usual advertisements. The latter are priced in dollars and sterling in the *New York Journal*. The newspapers are on the whole pro-British until the years immediately leading up to the Declaration of Independence. The war has to be traced mainly through British newspapers because the Newspaper Library's holdings of United States titles for this period are fairly limited, though gaps in the collections are filled where the opportunity arises. Nevertheless visitors to the Library still admire items such as the facsimile issue of *Dunlap's Pennsylvania Packet* published in 1876 to commemorate the Congress's momentous decision to secede from British rule.

55 The defence of Mafeking during the second Boer War (1899–1900) by Lt Col Baden-Powell's forces is chronicled in the *Mafeking Mail* of the period. Like Vicksburg's *Daily Citizen* (see 9), the newspaper was published on any materials to hand, which included wrapping paper, and pages from account books. (*Mafeking Mail*, Special Siege Slip, 10 February 1900.)

56 The East India Company's official and semi-official notices were also printed in local ethnic languages to ensure the widest possible dissemination amongst the literate mercantile population. (*Supplement to the Calcutta Gazette*, 7 April 1785.)

58 The publishers of the *Peking Gazette* relied upon 'hawkers' to distribute their newspaper. The man was sketched by an artist from the *Illustrated London News* on a visit to China. (*Illustrated London News*, 22 March 1873.)

57 *facing page.* Symbolic wood-cuts and uneven type-setting are characteristics of these Jamaican slave-owners' advertisements. (*Royal Gazette*, 14 July 1781.)

The first Australian newspaper, the *Sydney Gazette*, made its debut in 1803. When gold and silver were discovered, the Australian mining communities of Gympie and Geraldton proved to the world that they had become respectable places by publishing their own newspapers, the *Gympie Miner* and the *Geraldton Advertiser*. Emigrants seeking a new start in Australia may have been surprised to see *Bell's Life in Melbourne and Illustrated Sporting Gazette*, or the *Melbourne Punch* which closely copied their London equivalents, on sale on their arrival. To relieve the tedium of the journey from Britain to the Antipodes, one group of emigrants produced a newspaper called the *Albertland Gazette*, which was 'printed by Samuel Johnson in 35:30N lat. and 13:35W long.' on 14 June 1862. The Library's facsimile contains a list of passengers' names and details of their life aboard the 'Matilda Wattenbach'. This type of information was only occasionally reprinted in the pages of mainland newspapers.

Other lists of names can be seen in the *Royal Gazette* of 14 July 1781; but these are less pleasant reminders of the past, being lists of slaves who had run away or were to be sold at auction (**57**). This was a common feature of Caribbean newspapers at this time.

From the slaves' original homelands came stories of wars and struggles against Africans. The efforts made by European colonial

Montego-Bay, June 15, 1781.

FOR SALE, on Friday the 29th inst. in the harbour of Por Maria, the Atalanta's entire cargo of 416 prime Gold-Coast SLAVES, which was advertised for the 13th inst. at this place, but obliged to be put off for want of purchasers, on account of the present scarcity of provisions.

Mures & Dunlop.

☞ The Atalanta will sail this day, with the fleet to windward, under convoy of the Jamaica and go.

St. Ann's, June 14, 1781.

FOR SALE, forty or more able, seasoned, Field Negro Men and Women, six Carpenters and Mill-Wrights, and two Taylors; who have all had the small pox, and most of them have had the yaws.—For particulars, apply to RICHARD GRANT, Esq At-y at Law in Kingston, or of Mr. WILLIAM ROSON, the Proprietor, in St. Ann's:—Who also sell his PENN, called THATCHFIELD, the Remainder of the Negroes, and the Stock on, on reasonable Terms.

Moortown Estate, Manchione i, May 21, 1781.

RUN AWAY from Charles Bryan, jun. Esq; a Creole Negro Boy named

J O H N,

About 5 feet six inches high, is a common Waiting Man, and was dressed, when he absconded, a live y ruffin frock richly lined and trimed up with yellow, and a tuck of ash coloured cloth below lined. He is a markable small Black, has a scar on his forehead occasioned from the kick of a horse, which fractured it; he speaks very good English, and has been in England; it is therefore expected he will pass for a free man, and endeavour to get off in some of the next fleet: This is therefore to forewarn all captains of ships from taking him off the island. A reward of FIVE POUNDS will be given to who will secure him in any of the goals, by applying to Mr. West and Austin, merchants in Kingston, or the Subscriber.

CHARLES BRYAN, Junr.

Kingston, July 6th, 1781.

RAN AWAY, about a month since, a more negro-ish out fellow named GLASGOW, belonging to Mr. Hugh Polson, and was lately hired to Mr. Swarbreck. Any person bringing him to the subscriber, shall receive a pistole reward.

John Simpson.

June 29th, 1781.

Two Pounds Fifteen Shillings Reward.

RUN AWAY,

From the subscriber, about 10 days past, a mulatto woman named HARRIET, and her child, named MARY; she is suspected to be gone to some part of wind-ward. Any person that will bring the said mulattoes to the subscriber in Royal, shall receive the above reward; or if any can prove by whom either of them is harboured, besides the above reward, be handsomely rewarded, so that the offender or offenders may be brought to justice.

Moses Mendes Sollas.

Kingston, 24th February, 1781.

RUN AWAY,

the 26th of November last, A NEGRO MAN, named

S A M,

He is a Creole born, a very stout, able well-made Negro, about five feet, eight inches high, very black skin, low forehead, and thick neck; he is capable of being a Waiting Man, a Cook, a Sailor, and almost every thing you can set him about: In the planting, fencing, and railing business he can handle the adz and saw pretty well, though left-handed. He is very well acquainted with almost every part of the Island, and absented himself before for a considerable time, and said he was then with the Maroon Negroes. He is very fond of gaming, and is often in parties of idle fellows, beating cotter, &c. and is supposed to be some where about Spanish-Town, or Kingston. Whoever will apprehend said Negro, and deliver him to the subscriber, or secure him in any gaol of this Island, giving information thereof to the subscriber, shall receive FIVE POUNDS reward from

RICHARD MILES.

Kingston, 22d December, 1780.

WANTED immediately, to lease or hire, for six or twelve eighteen months, or two years certain, from ten to fifteen able

FIELD NEGROES,

who have been used to Plantation Work.—They are to be employed in Liguanea, cutting fire wood, and making Lime.—The hire will be paid quarterly, in Cash or Navy Bills.—Any person that has such Negroes to dispose of, will please apply to

JAMES STEINSON}
At his Lime-house in Kingston. }

Kingston, 2d June, 1781.

RUN AWAY

From the subscriber about six weeks ago, a Sambo man slave named GEORGE, lately the property of Mr. Gotchal Lemon, marked on one or both his shoulders G. L.—by trade a barber. He is supposed to be harboured by his relations at Mr. Craddock's mountain, in St. John's. If he does not immediately return, the Maroon negroes will be sent out to apprehend him; and a reward of Five Pound will be given to any person who will bring him to the subscriber, or lodge him in any of the gaols of this island.

E. B. LOUSADA.

N. B. As he will probably attempt to get off the island, all Captains of vessels are hereby cautioned against receiving him on board; as they will be prosecute to the utmost rigour of the law.

Kingston, 26th May, 1781.

T A K E N U P,

At Spring-Valley Penn, 3d inst.

TWO

NEW NEGROES;

One of them says his name is

DERRY.

Five feet nine inches high, a shot lodged in his left shoulder and a scar on his breast. The other calls himself DANIEL, has filed teeth, but no scar or mark, both of the Mundingo country; They say they did belong to some gentlemen who had Frenchmen; one of them is lame or he should have been sent to goal.

JAMES BROWN, Sen.

Annotto-Bay, April 7, 1781.

RUN AWAY,

LAST NOVEMBER, A Creole Negro man, named

CASTALIO,

(but going by the name of) H. was formerly the property of Susanna Ogier, and is bound to William Mure, late of the Parish of St. George, Carpenter, and now to his hire. He was taken into custody, and in taking him over to his parish he made his escape and has since been heard of. He lives by Water, where his mother lives, or bringing in Kingston being bred here to that business. He is a middle aged fellow, of a very low complexion, has a small lump over his right eye. Whoever apprehends the said Negro and confines him in any workhouse, or brings him to the subscriber, in the parish of St. George, shall receive TWO PISTOLES reward, and whoever will discover by whom harboured or concealed, shall, on conviction of the offender, receive TEN PISTOLES reward.

DAVID SUTHERLAND.

Manchieal, June 4, 1781.

RUN AWAY from the Subscriber, a Negro Boy named TOM, marked on the right shoulder P S, about five foot eight, stout made.

Whoever will bring him to the Subscriber, or secure him in any of the island, shall be entitled to Two Pistoles Reward, from

PAT. SPINK.

Seed Grove, 8th June 1781.

TO BE SOLD at Public Vendue at Annotto Bay, the 1st of August next for Cash or good Bills of Exchange,

15 seasoned Field Negroes used to Jobbing; also a Mustee SHADY GROVE PENN, in the Parish of St. George:—viz, 28 good Field Negroes, with the whole of SHADY GROVE, containing 300 Acres, bounding on Spanish River.—The Land is very easy, and well adapted for a Breeding and Fattening Penn, having about 60 acres of very fine Pasture, well fenced, with a few Breeding stock then on, and plenty of Provisions.—There needed on the Premise a new framed Dwelling House newly finished, with Out Office, &c—and the Land bound with Cedar, and other house timbers.—The whole sold, time will be given for the greatest part of the purchase money; if only the 28 Negroes, immediate payment is expected.—For further Particulars, enquire of WILLIAM Ross, Esq; Richmond, St. Mary's or Messrs. Ru ert M'Kay, John Sanderson, or James Anderson St. George's

Kingston, May 18, 1781.

For Charter,

The Brigantine

MARTHA,

A stout British-built vessel, Burthen 120 Tons.

FOR TERMS, APPLY TO

Cuninghame & Ballantyne:

Who have for Sale the following Articles, imported in said Brigantine, viz
Superfine FLOUR in barrels | Split BEANS in bags
Fine BARLEY in kegs | CORDAGE, &c.

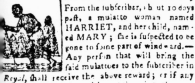

emigrants to expand as far and as quickly as possible across new lands were often violently opposed by the indigenous populations. Reports of conflict, uprisings and widespread mutiny were sent back to England. The modern-day reader will be forgiven for thinking that the British were always at war during Victoria's reign, if the reports in *The Graphic* or the *Illustrated London News* are to be believed. In essence, the 'pax britannica' was a series of short wars which involved the spreading of European civilisation and Christianity at the point of a bayonet. The home reader could be kept abreast of the latest heroic deeds of the British Army.

Some of these exploits are worthy of mention. Colonel Baden-Powell's spirited and imaginative defence of Mafeking during the Second Boer War of 1899–1900 can be followed in the *Mafeking Mail Special Siege Slip*, 'printed daily, shells permitting' (55). Like the Vicksburg *Daily Citizen*, this was published on anything to hand – including pages from a foolscap accounts book, wrapping paper and note-paper. The daily issues carry stories of the war, courts-martial, puzzles and entertainment.

If these events are familiar to many readers, it is likely that others which took place in South-East Asia are not. Some are recorded in the pages of the *North China Mail* from Shanghai or the *Kobe Chronicle* from Japan, published for the European community. Others are only accessible with a knowlege of Chinese, Japanese or other Oriental languages.

Newspapers are designed to be thrown away, and it is human nature to want something once it has gone. The true passing of time can be appreciated by the serious modern-day reader only when he is confronted with the photograph of the young boy and the elderly man who is looking for the photograph. Small paragraphs which are usually overlooked take on a great significance for someone who has long sought them. Over the years that newspapers have been printed, great events have been recorded along with these 'insignificant' occurrences. Thus the awful devastation caused by the atomic 'bomb that changed the world' will appear on the front page, and a happy reunion or marriage on the inside pages. As long as people wish to find an opinion which coincides with their own, or indeed an alternative, newspapers will be sold in large numbers, whilst newsboys encourage us to 'Read all about it!'.

Suggestions for further reading

BRITISH LIBRARY Reference Division *Signs of the Times: the 200th anniversary* (exhibition notes). – London: British Library, 1985

HUTT, Alan *The changing newspaper: typographic trends in Britain and America, 1622–1972*. – London: Gordon Fraser, 1973

JACKSON, Mason *Illustrated News: a sketch of the rise and progress of pictorial journalism*. In *Illustrated London News* 4 Jan.–30 Aug. 1879

LEE, Alan J *The origins of the popular press, 1885–1914*. – London: Croom Helm, 1976

MORAN, James *Printing presses: history and development from the fifteenth century to modern times*. – London: Faber & Faber, 1973

NEVETT, T R *Advertising in Britain: a history*. – London: Heinemann, 1982